STRESS RX

103 Prescriptions for Overcoming Stress and Achieving Lifelong Happiness

Edwin Riley, Ph.D.

Edwin Riley Ph.D.
241 Mercury Circle, Ste 4
Juno Beach, FL 33408
561.628.8007
www.stressreduction.com

Cover Photo by Edwin Riley

DISCLAIMER: The nutritional and health information provided in this book is intended for educational purposes only. Nothing listed or mentioned in this book should be considered as medical advice or a substitute for medical advice for dealing with stress or any other medical problem. Consult your health-care professional for individual guidance on specific health issues and before following this or any program. Persons with serious medical conditions should seek professional care. The author and publisher specifically disclaim any liability, loss or risk, personal or otherwise, which is incurred as a consequence, directly or indirectly, of the use and application of the contents of this book.

www.stressreduction.com

Praise for Edwin Riley's

Stress Rx

"I love *"Stress Rx"*! In it you will discover the importance of mindful eating and the connection between our food choices and our state of well being. It is sure to illuminate."   *– Mark Reinfeld, Co-author, Vegan Fusion World Cuisine, The Complete Idiot's Guide to Eating Raw, and the 30-minute Vegan. Kapaau, Hawaii*

"Stress Rx" represents the life work of Edwin Riley with its twists and turns, textured dimensions and extraordinary insights. Only a professional with acute perception can write as directly and powerfully as this book displays."

- *Dr. Brian Clements, Director Hippocrates Healing Institute, West Palm Beach, FL*

"Edwin Riley is a virtuoso educator with a power-filled healing message for working through and transcending stress. From every direction and in an unending onslaught we are up to our eyeballs in stress and its effects on dealing with stress. His intensive background as a creative writer, provolutionary poet, surfer on the literary breakers of liberated philosophy, energy therapist, and rare cross-trained doctor in mind-body integration/health issues altogether gives his message of *""Stress Rx""* a razor-edged relevance. He can help you!"

- *Wilbur Curless, Ph.D., Florida Atlantic University, Boca Raton, FL*

"The best thing about *"Stress Rx"* is that it is much, much more than a guide for dealing with life's stress. It is rather a fundamental guide to rich, full living. It includes excellent advice for improving relationships, creating personal inner peace and becoming successful. It combines the wisdom of good psychology, spirituality and just plain common sense into a mélange that can be helpful to anyone. I was particularly struck by his willingness to include a comprehensive chapter on sexuality which too often is ignored in such works. I also enjoyed his "103 prescriptions" which allows anyone to find cogent suggestions to address almost any life issue. It is thus a useful handbook for anyone in today's fast-paced and challenging world. Well done, Edwin!"   *- Rev. R. Scott Sherman, Unity Minister; founder of EnVision Ministries.*

"Even though Dr. Hans Selye is unequivocally the father of stress research, Sir William Osler, the father of American Medicine, wrote over 100 years ago that many illnesses are the result of our stress-filled lives. Despite this knowledge and the hundreds of books dealing with stress, a majority of Americans remain stressed. The time has long passed for a common sense solution to the stress-illness continuum. Edwin Riley's *"Stress Rx"* offers everyone an excellent opportunity to reach inside to their own hidden talent for healing and enjoying life. The time has come for all good people to take care of themselves and manage their stress!"   *- C. Norman Shealy, M.D., Ph.D., Professor of Energy Medicine, President Emeritus, Holos University Graduate Seminary, Founding President, American Holistic Medical Association.*

"By reading this text all will benefit greatly, enhance their life experience and extend their time on the planet. Following Dr. Riley's axioms is also an elixir in the pursuit of happiness."   - *Samuel James Freas Ed.D., Author, Screenwriter, and former Olympic and Collegiate Coach. Palm Beach Gardens, FL*

"A spectacular book such as this will greatly contribute to a less stressful society."

- *Dr. Yang, Jwing-Ming, Author of 38 books on chi kung and the martial arts; Founder of 45 schools around the world, Boston, MA*

"*Stress Rx*" is a valuable self-healing book that beautifully addresses the issues to modern stress in a way that is both uplifting and practical. It helps create the awareness space for the ultimate dissolving of stress in one's life which is to know the unlimited, non-casual joy, peace, love and contentment of knowing the true self." - *Rebbe Gabriel Cousens, M.D., Director of the Tree of Life Rejuvenation Center and author of Creating Peace By Being Peace, Patagonia, Arizona.*

About Dr. Edwin Riley, PH.D, M.ED.

Edwin Riley is a doctor of Mind/Body Medicine, Transpersonal Psychology, and Integrative Health Care. In addition to his private practice in Palm Beach County, Florida, he periodically conducts "Stress Reduction Vacations" in the tropical mountains outside Cuernavaca, Mexico. He also lectures extensively throughout the United States on topics related to stress reduction, anti-aging, and the mind/body connection, helping people facing difficulties gain control over fear and stress.

A proponent of natural healing for 30 years, he completed his doctoral internship under the direction of Dr. Jon Kabat-Zinn at the nationally acclaimed Center for Mindfulness in Medicine, Health Care, and Society at the University of Massachusetts Medical Center. He is certified as a Hippocrates Health Educator and also lectures on enzyme nutrition, the bio-chemistry of foods, and exercise physiology. Dr. Riley received his Master's degree at the University of Florida. He taught creative writing and communications in colleges and universities, and currently conducts workshops in Healing Chi Kung and tai chi, both in the United States and Mexico.

His unique combination of skills as a journalist, professor, therapist and speaker give him the ability to simplify difficult concepts, allowing people to put them to use successfully in their daily lives. He also served as Director of the South Florida Stress Reduction Institute in West Palm Beach, Florida.

Dr. Riley's research led him to the curanderos and shamanic healers in Mexico where he accessed centuries-old holistic healing traditions. In November 2002, Dr. Riley began living in Mexico part of the year where he facilitates week-long stress reduction vacations. He is also engaged in a research project with a plant that promotes nutritional and medicinal benefits.

For an upcoming schedule, an outline of Dr. Riley's programs, or to contact him directly visit his website at www.stressreduction.com.

FORWARD- **STRESS RX**

"Stress Rx" represents the life work of Dr. Edwin Riley with its twists and turns, textured dimensions and extraordinary insights. Only a professional with acute perception can write as directly and powerfully as this book displays. In this high-speed insane world that is more focused on economic survival than human dimensions, we all suffer great loss daily. Whatever happened to the concept, "work to life?" It has certainly become, "Live to Work."

For most people, their passionate desires were squelched at a young age and they now find themselves drowning in responsibilities that they do not favor. I have worked for four decades with those battling catastrophic disease and can assure you that stress is at the center of the cause. There is no better way to devastate your immune system than to have gnawing destructive thoughts pervade your consciousness.

Furthermore, most people feel out of control since the basis for their own survival has never been taught to them nor have they applied it. Replacing simple acts with grandiose ideology seems to be the path that most humans take. Dr. Riley, however, guides you back to yourself, while slowly handing your life back to you. From his vast experience, he will teach you those things that you did not learn as a child in your family setting or social normalties. When consistently applied, the wisdom and techniques described in *"Stress Rx"* will help you bring about a sense of stability and control that will help to alleviate the self-imposed stresses created from your lack of confidences.

All the problems we experience today initiate from the fear that we must resolve. Resolution is the only mechanism that brings about a new sense of self which in turn abolishes insecurity. Forthright living and concrete convictions are rare among the stressed, but prevalent among the successful.

Edwin Riley is right on target by subtitling the book, achieving life-long happiness. Happiness is an emotion you were born with, and in abundance. Slowly but surely, it slipped away as you replaced your passion and purpose with problems and limitation. In his offering, he speaks about the ripple effect. The effect quite often becomes a tidal wave that engulfs your very existence. There is no doubt that those of you reading this powerful publication will receive more than you expected. But this is only the first step. Taking the key messages in this text from concept to personal realization will assuredly free you from melancholy and offer you a floral bouquet of possibilities.

Be Well,
Dr. Brian Clement, Ph.D.,L.N.,N.D.
Hippocrates Health Institute

TABLE OF CONTENTS

ACKNOWLEDGEMENTS

Each of us is unique; each of us has a distinct voiceprint, footprint, fingerprint and DNA.

Even our personal journey in life has its own exclusive imprint. *"Stress Rx"* is my imprint; in these pages I will share my interconnectedness with you and the other souls that inhabit this earth.

I will share other people's stories, so if your experiences are similar you will know you are not alone. We all want an assurance that we're not alone, that our problems are not unique and that we are not drifting out to sea without a lifeboat. That's why I created this safe port in the storm of life. Think of this book as your umbrella or flotation device. It aims to heal whatever ails you.

I would like to offer my special thanks to Jon Kabat-Zinn, Director emeritus of the Center for Mindfulness in the Department of Medicine at the University of Massachusetts (UM). Some of the exercises in *"Stress Rx"* were initially discovered during my doctoral internship at UM. It is there that I learned the necessity of taking responsibility for one's own healing.

Thanks to Saki Santorelli, successor to Jon Kabat-Zinn as director of the stress reduction program and to the entire staff for their patience, encouragement and endless hours in dialogue on the multi-faceted subject of stress.

I want to recognize Yang Jwing-Ming for his enlightening children's story about Hou-Yi, Master Shou-Yu Liang for his Qi Permeating chi kung form, and Sifu Wei Lun Huang for his 17 years of instruction in both tai chi and chi kung that taught me the necessity for being grounded.

My immense gratitude to the friends who continue to support and encourage me with unconditional love: Sri David Rebmann, Dr. Steve Driscoll, Dr. Wilbur Curless, Neil Robinson, Rainbow Rick. J.W. Allen, Patricia Hueze, Alejandro Villanueva, Drs. Brian and Anna Maria Clement, Dr. Lawrence Reid, Malcolm Kirschenbaum, Gabriel Cousens, M.D., the late Edith Ross and William Meares and to other friends whom I do not mention but hold in spirit.

I also wish to recognize those past and present whom I've had the privilege to meet and who have influenced my search for meaningfulness in life: Norman Mailer, Jimmy Breslin, Ram Dass, Thich Nhat Hanh, Swamis Satchidananda and Muktananda, the notorious Hunter S. Thompson, and the "King" himself, Elvis Presley.

I want to recognize my dad for his love of nature and my 89-year-old mother for being the dreamer that she still is; my brothers, Les and Roy, and my children, Kimila Ann and Trey, who continue to teach me the meaning of patience and love. May my grandchildren Ricky, Drew, and Katelyn discover their own inner voices and express themselves with loving kindness. And finally, to my paternal and maternal grandparents – farmers and city folk – who loved me and provided a balance of normalcy not found in textbooks.

I also want to thank the many people who confided their deep secrets to me. Thanks to Sharon Ann Carrick for her tedious hours transcribing tapes, Janeen Serino for e-book formatting and to L.A. Justice for the editorial assistance and inspiration that enabled me to bring completion to the initial manuscript.

This book was made possible through the trials and tribulations of my life experiences. After surviving a thousand stressful related deaths, I feel qualified to offer advice on how to reduce stress and cope successfully in order to master the goal of inner peace and tranquility.

From a place of gratitude and love,

Edwin Riley
November 2008

INTRODUCTION

The Equal Opportunity Condition – STRESS

Stress is a condition that affects everyone. If you walk the earth, then you have probably been afflicted by the universal condition known as stress.

The good news is that you were given the gift of life, and the bad news is that with this gift (which is nonrefundable) come challenges. There is no escape hatch, no getaway car and no stunt man to handle them for you.

That's the beauty of our existence – it comes with a lifetime guarantee of unending challenges. And the best part, you get to choose how to deal with them. You can resolve them with equanimity and patience (the happily-ever-after script) and be at peace with the world. Or you can swim upstream, fighting the people, places and things that get in your way of how things should be.

Just remember that stress is a part of everyone's life – whether rich or poor, famous or unknown, brilliant or simple, spectacularly beautiful or homely. But what makes the difference between a happy life and a difficult one is our perception of and reaction to life's events, not the event itself.

That is why I created this book – to share the secret of creating lifelong happiness. "Stress Rx" is also a stress survival guide. It will carry you through those difficult and challenging times when you are surrounded by darkness. It is your personal "get-out-of-chaos" card when your life seems insurmountable and your loved ones seem temporarily insane.

The exercises, questionnaires and anecdotes in this book are appropriate for men and women, young and old – and you know why? Because stress is an equal-opportunity condition. Some of us were lucky and had good role models for coping with adversity. Some of us were not.

But one thing I can guarantee: It is how you relate and respond to stress that defines the quality of your life. And if the sages are right when they say "treat every day as if it is your last," then you might want to climb on board now; a day of stress and strain is one less perfect day in the calendar of your life.

A Manual for Surviving Stress

This book is a stress survival manual. It was written with you in mind. The quizzes, exercises, and other material are meant to heal all who enter. Chances are if you have this book in your hand, then you are the perfect person to benefit from its intelligence and wisdom.

One interesting thing to know about stress is that it was originally created as a protective device. When the cave man was out looking for food he would often encounter wild animals. To alert his body to the dangers that lurked, the cerebral cortex (in the emotional ecosystem) would light up, causing a heightened feeling (or adrenaline rush) called "fight or flight." The caveman had a choice: stake his claim and battle it out, or run for his life. Today, we may not have to run from a saber tooth tiger, but we might have a stressful job (or no job), prolonged illness, difficult relationships, hectic 24/7 existence or just too many e-mails to deal with.

If you are burdened by the cumulative effects of stress, your body may stay primed for a fight. This works well for firefighters at the scene of a blaze, but for the average person this state of being is not something you can afford. It can cause headaches, nausea, insomnia, fearfulness, panic or illness, and – if prolonged – serious disease.

Stress also has the potential to affect your interpersonal relationships. Sex experts have long believed that stress can lower the libido, therefore putting additional stress on intimate relationships and marriages (and even causing the demise of some.)

Over time this vicious cycle can wreak havoc on the body. It can cause coronary disease, ulcers, sadness, depression, anxiety attacks or chronic fatigue syndrome. People who live in a high state of anxiety are five times as likely to die of a heart attack or stroke. Medical experts estimate that 80- to 95-percent of illness is stress - related.

A 2007 survey by the American Psychological Association found that 62 percent of people said their work caused undue stress in their lives. Seventy-three percent said financial concerns were the number-one factor affecting their stress levels. That is why it is vital to learn coping techniques and exercises to alleviate stress in your life. Stress may be a given in our contemporary culture, but it doesn't have to wipe out the joy and fulfillment in your life. That's what his book is for – to take you on a journey to health and wellness not stress and disease. Remember, it is not what happens to you in life, but how you see and respond to it.

The Culture Vulture – STRESS

Stress related illness is not solely an American phenomenon. In Australia, over 50,000 people are admitted to the hospital each year for treatment of severe stress. The British Department of Health reports that the average age of stress-related hospitalization is 38 for both men and women; the average stay is 18 days.

While we all feel anxious at times, constant anxiety can severely disrupt our lives. It might rear its head as a phobia, obsessive thought patterns, compulsive behavior or panic attacks. A panic attack can be a frightening experience, causing symptoms such as rapid heartbeat, trembling, sweating, feelings of terror, throat constriction, dizziness, chest pains and tingling in the extremities.

The Far Side of Stress – What Happens When Stress is Left Unchecked

In some instances extreme stress can cause the demise of one's career – and one's life. Take Hunter S. Thompson, for example. This extremely accomplished author and journalist had everything going for him. He wrote the best-selling novel *Fear and Loathing in Las Vegas,* which later became a popular movie starring Johnny Depp. Thompson was also credited with pioneering gonzo journalism. But it wasn't enough – Thompson wasn't happy. In fact, he was a deeply troubled man.

I learned firsthand. It was my idea to ferry Mr. Thompson to Miami to speak at the International Book Fair. Although everyone in command of the event was against picking Thompson because of his reputation to erratic behavior and for abusing drugs and alcohol, I wanted to hear from the legendary writer who had written for Rolling Stone and Playboy magazines.

But I quickly learned that Thompson was more than even I could handle (dealing with stress compounded by self-destruction is a lethal combination). He was pretty much out of it when he landed at the airport and barely even knew what day it was. Shortly after arriving he pulled a disappearing act; I found him at the bar downing a margarita and some scotch while simultaneously consuming coffee and an ice-cream bar. Once in the car with me, he began spooning a white substance into his nose. He became extremely paranoid and reluctant to speak to the audience of people that were in attendance at the Miami Book Fair. When Thompson finally did get up to address the group his voice was garbled and his delivery was not on par with our intellectually curious audience. I was concerned by his extreme methods for handling stress and the level of dysfunction that resulted.

When I was told not to let this prolific writer out of my sight (by his New York agent) I couldn't believe his demons could be that bad. But I found out they were much worse than I expected. On the way to the airport at 7 a.m. the next morning, I asked him to autograph my worn copy of *Fear and Loathing in Las Vegas* after telling him, "I don't think you'll be around much longer." Hunter laughed, took the book, and inscribed it, "Edwin, thanks for getting me to the goddamn airport on time."

That was the last time I saw Thompson. At 5:42 p.m. on February 20, 2005 – 16 years later – in Woody Creek, Colorado, he died from a self-inflicted gunshot wound to the head. Although an extreme example of what happens when stress is not dealt with – and even fueled to escalate – Thompson was living proof that intense anxiety and self-abuse can be a lethal combination.

After the Fact – The Stressful Life

Although Thompson was known to have panic attacks, he self-medicated them with alcohol and multiple drugs. That's why it is important to understand what a panic attack looks and feels like. A panic attack can sometimes feel like a heart attack, and you think you are dying. These attacks are usually followed by a feeling of despair or depression, accompanied by irrational thoughts that it will happen again.

Why does the body respond physically to emotional anxiety? Well, our stress response is triggered by the mind; fearful or worrisome thoughts produce a chemical reaction in the body. When this fight-or-flight response is invoked by a situation that we see as threatening, the hormones cortisol and epinephrine (also known as adrenaline) are released into the blood-stream. When this happens, the heart beats faster, blood pressure soars, the muscles tense and the extremities might feel cold and clammy.

The good news, however, is that stress disorders can be treated and eliminated. Studies show that stress management programs and techniques like the ones in this book can help people relax, thereby reducing the risk of heart attack – and other ailments – by 72 percent! *"Stress Rx"* is your prescription for success; it can help break the cycle of anxiety-related disorders and help you heal yourself. While no one is ever completely free of stress (except perhaps for brief periods while lounging on a beach in the Bahamas), you can learn how to manage stress and enjoy more in life.

The Road Map to Relaxation: Stepping Up

Life can be a pressure cooker, with stress as a primary ingredient. It is increasingly important therefore that we learn how to handle this insidious challenger. Having experienced many stressful situations myself, and having witnessed the negative effects of stress on other people's lives, I became inspired to help others cope more effectively with stress.

To accomplish this goal, I teamed up with some excellent doctors to create The South Florida Stress Reduction Clinic, which was modeled after a program by the Center for Mindfulness, Medicine, Health Care, and Society at the University of Massachusetts Medical Center. The techniques taught at the clinic became the core material for this book, and over the years I developed a step-by-step program that will help you attain a more relaxed approach to life.

The program includes breathing techniques and exercises that reduce muscular tension and restore mental focus. By incorporating these simple relaxation techniques into your daily routine, you can attain a sense of mastery and relaxation.

What I found among patients at the clinic – regardless of their socio-economic background, age or medical diagnosis – was a perception that stress was a defining part of their life. They believed their lives were stressful. But, once we challenged and shifted their perceptions (through the application of these practices) they were able to slow down, take a better look at their lives, and begin living with renewed exhilaration.

The patients were then able to accept full responsibility for their health and well-being. They were able to see that their illness or dysfunction was created by how they were interpreting their life situations. This learning freed them from the shackles of disease and opened up the avenues of healing. When we realize that we can control our destiny, then our destiny is guided by our dreams, not our nightmares.

If you want to make the most of life's journey with the least amount of stress, then regard this book as your valued tour guide.

If you have a physical problem causing severe stress, or if you want to prevent unwanted disease from occurring, put these tools into practice and transform your life.

Some of you may already be doing your best to reduce stress by exercising regularly, meditating and eating healthy foods. That is an excellent start. But if you want to move through blockages that are preventing your joy and happiness, then jump in and read on, or visit my website; www.stressreduction.com. While it might be challenging at first, it gets easier with practice. As they say, the best things in life are worth it.

Chapter 1

From Here to Eternity

"Do not dwell in the past; do not dream of the future,
Concentrate the mind on the present moment." - Buddha

A quiz: HOW STRESSED ARE YOU?

Take a moment to answer this short quiz to get insight into your current stress level. Be honest with yourself; this is the first step in turning your life around. Within the past 12 months....

1.   Have you lost a spouse, child or parent?

Yes or No

2.   Are you going through a separation or divorce?

Yes or No

3.   Have you ended a long term relationship?

Yes or No

4.   Involved in a serious accident or have a serious illness?

Yes or No

5.   Did you get married or are you planning a wedding?

Yes or No

6. Have you started a new job?

Yes or No

7. Were you fired from a job?

Yes or No

8. Have you retired?

Yes or No

9. Have you had a baby (or a multiple birth)?

Yes or No

10. Have you moved?

Yes or No

11. Is your house in foreclosure?

Yes or No

12. Have you lost significant investment monies?

Yes or No

KEY: If you answered yes to four or more of these questions, your anxiety level is already at maximum level. That means you need to stop what you are doing and find ways to reduce the stress that often accompanies these events. Following a path of hardship can be dangerous to one's health. Our bodies tell us when we are in a danger zone. Pay attention to the signs, and put consistent practices in place now to avoid physical breakdown. Now is the time to rethink your life and your coping mechanisms.

If you answered yes to one or two of these questions, then be careful not to add anything stressful into your life at the moment. It may be a good time to practice saying no to requests that are not a priority. One thing about stress is that it can build, and before you know it you're out of control. Stay close to your heart, pay attention to your thoughts, and see what patterns you are falling into that may be causing stress.

If you answered no to all these questions, then sit back, relax and enjoy this book. You will be glad you did. Life is always changing; learning how to reduce stress now will prepare you for when the challenges come. One word of caution: Although you may not be facing a major life challenge right now, you may also not be happy. In this case, it would be helpful to evaluate what is really going on with your life. Have you resigned yourself to a situation or relationship in life that is causing you unhappiness? Are you avoiding changes that you want to make because you fear the unknown? Chronic unhappiness due to a life of inaction is also a cause of stress, and it can adversely affect our health. If you are avoiding changes that need to be made, then seek the help of a coach or counselor to help while incorporating the tools and exercises in this book. Most of you already know that stress is a necessary part of life and of human existence, and that it is often our greatest teacher. So get on board and grab a paddle.

Becoming a 'Master Archer'

Most of us are looking for something new – something that will make our lives just a little bit better. We hunger for that illusive peace of mind, yet we are not sure how to get there.

Yet, for many of us this search for calm ends up being the road very well-traveled – the one in motion. We shift gears continuously as we drive, bike, fly and walk and as we tend to the little things that make up our daily existence.

At times it seems like nothing is simple. Everything we do and every situation we encounter is fraught with complications, challenges, and problems (no, you're not alone here). So how do we get from here – a place of anticipation and anxiety – to there – a place of peace and calm?

That's the journey that we are taking now. As you will read shortly, it will be like the journey taken by the Master Archer. His travels took him ten years to complete, but I promise that yours won't take as long. And how do I know? Because I've seen it happen for those who take this practice to heart.

The Master Archer

Hou-Yi was a young man whose ambition was to become a world class archer. That meant that he had to travel far and wide to get close to his goal. He walked and walked and hitched rides from strangers for three months. When he arrived at the door of the Master Archer, he said "I'm Hou-Yi. I have come a long distance to learn what you have to teach me."

The Master Archer shook his hand sadly and said, "I am sorry, I am not taking on any new students."

Although Hou-Yi pleaded earnestly, he was turned away. But Hou-Yi was determined to stay until the Master Archer relented. He sat for one day, then two days straight. On the third day it snowed so the Master Archer opened his door and said: "I am impressed by your determination, but there are three things you must do for me."

12

Hou-Yi jumped up joyfully and bowed. "Yes, yes, anything." "First, go home and every day for the next three years light an incense stick," said the Master. "Then come back to see me."

Hou-Yi went home and lit incense sticks, but he was fidgety and restless. He wanted to be an archer, not an incense burner. As the years went by, he found himself becoming calmer and focused. Lighting the sticks became a pleasure instead of a chore.

When Hou-Yi returned to the Master's house three years later, the Archer was pleased. He looked at Hou-Yi and said: "For the next three years, watch your wife weave on the loom. Then, come back and tell me what you have learned."

At home, Hou-Yi watched the loom, his eyes darting back and forth with the shuttle until he was overcome with dizziness. As the years went by he felt one with the shuttle, until it seemed to move so slowly he could see every thread.

When he appeared at the home of the Master Archer again he was told to go home and weave ten baskets a day. Because Hou-Yi knew that even the best basket weavers could produce only three baskets a day, he felt the task was impossible and that he would fail. Hou-Yi's progress was slow at first but as the years went on, he went from two baskets a day – to 10 – to 15. By the time he went to the Master Archer's home for the fourth time he was accomplished in many ways.

"It is good to see you," said the Master Archer, "but you have learned all I can teach you."

Hou-Yi was baffled and angry. He reached into his quiver and pulled out an arrow. He pulled back the bow string determined to shoot the Archer's hat off. Without turning around the Master snapped a bow from his own quiver and shot Hou-Yi's arrow down in mid air.

The duel of arrows was repeated again. On the third try, Hou-Yi knew he would be victorious because the Master was out of arrows. Suddenly, the Master's hand shot up, snapped off a young willow branch, loaded his bow and shot down Hou-Yi's arrow in mid air.

Hou-Yi hung his head and said "I understand. What you cannot teach me is experience."

Practice Makes Perfect…Usually

What we can learn from the Master Archer is that experience only comes from practice. There are no shortcuts, no magic pills and no quick fixes for learning to cope with stress. However, there are ways to integrate body and mind to reduce the effects of stressful situations that can so easily take over your life.

Like Hou-Yi, many of us want instant gratification. We want to arrive at our destination sooner than we are ready. And like Hou-Yi, want to cut out those who stand in our way. But as Hou-Yi learned to accept and enjoy his duties as an apprentice, he learned valuable lessons that gave his life meaning. This same thing can happen to you.

You will find that changing your lifestyle will lead to less stress in your life. Not only that, you will be opening the door to a renewed life that incorporates one of wisdom and joy.

Only you can make this transformation. Only you can move from here, a place of stress, to there, a place that is closer to the blissful state of the Master Archer.

These pages are full of stories from people who felt as though they had lost control over their lives, who used pills, food, alcohol, sex and drugs to help them get through the day. By taking this journey you will learn how to transform your life in the same way they did. You will see that this way of life is a win-win (a slam-dunk, actually), and no one loses.

Listen to Your Body – If it Talks, Listen

Rx #1: Whatever the mind can conceive, the body can usually achieve. Even if you are riddled with pain and are stressed out, you can learn to be peaceful, pain-free and relaxed once you've mastered a few simple techniques.

If you're reading this book, then chances are you see the value in being calm. You may also have an interest in letting go of the need for anti-anxiety drugs such as Xanax, Valium, Ativan, and Paxil. Sadly, pharmaceutical companies are making huge sums of money because, as a society, we are burdened by stress from financial problems, unhealthy relationships and jobs we may not like. Very often, people's lives are like steaming pots on a hot stove, ready to bubble over. Or perhaps you're on a slow simmer steaming your energy away.

Jeff was an accountant who took early retirement. He was well-off financially and spent most of his days golfing and playing cards with his friends in South Florida. If you saw Jeff, you would have thought that he had an ideal life. But one day everything changed. He came to me with a case of shingles; a painful rash caused by the chickenpox virus and often brought on by stress or anxiety.

His head was an inflamed ball of fire. "The pain is unbearable." He said. "I can't think or enjoy my life anymore. One day life was so much fun, and now I would rather be dead."

Jeff had portrayed himself as a happy-go-lucky guy just hitting the links and shuffling the deck. But in our clinical stress-reduction sessions he admitted to being concerned about his wife's dwindling health. Jeff was also worried about the emotional triggers that set off his rash. Most physical illnesses — according to leading medical authorities — have an underlying emotional imbalance. With this, stress arises like a phoenix from the ashes.

Jeff's voice cracked and his eyes reddened. "My Mind is shit," he told me. "The doctors tell me to relax. If I knew how to relax, don't you think I would be doing that? How can I relax when I have bleeding festers all over my head and the pain is unbearable? That's all I can think about. Nothing else matters."

Jeff's illness had become his new identity. His entire world revolved around his pain — it became the largest part of his persona.

"If you can see the pain as separate from who you are, then the pain becomes less important," I advised him. "Often, it will disappear on its own."

"That's easier said than done," Jeff told me. "How can I go out in public when everyone stares? How can I concentrate on my swing when I'm in agony?"

"But you're still a father, a husband, a good friend and a likeable guy with a problem that won't last forever," I told him. "It will pass, everything does."

Changing our perception, especially when confronted with physical discomfort, is never easy. But once you see that the illness really isn't who you are — but rather a passing situation — then you can move forward where transformation can take place. You will also no longer be defined by your illness. You will know that you are much larger and more powerful than this temporary problem.

As the weeks passed, Jeff's rash didn't go away. "It seems as though you're clinging to it, "I told him. "You've made it part of your life, and you need to accept it."

"Why should I accept it?" he asked angrily

"Because it's letting you know that you're stressed," I explained. "Just like a thermometer measures a fever, this rash is showing you that YOU have not learned to free yourself from what is causing the stress. Once you accept this and acknowledge that you need help, you will be able to respond properly to it and uncover the cause. But it takes awareness on your part."

I'm happy to say that after seven weeks of private sessions and practicing the stress-reduction techniques in this book, Jeff's shingles began to subside. He learned how to breathe, how to stay in the now, and how to manage the stress he felt about his family. Within a few months he was back to playing golf and cards, this time with greater awareness about how to handle the challenges in his life.

Alice, a thin wiry woman in her fifties, joined one of my stress-reduction groups. Her frizzy hair, which hung over her face, makes her appear to be hiding from something. She was a nervous bundle of energy, and during our eight-week session she found herself without a place to stay. Alice had also confided that she couldn't keep a job for very long.

"I'm sleeping at a friend's house but my things are stored with my sister," she told me. "I'm really frazzled, I feel disconnected and filled with stress."

"Your stress level would drop considerably if you could plan ahead," I suggested.

"I know I create my own stress. I apply for jobs that have long hours and I can't unwind and sleep. I feel overwhelmed most of the time, and I'm so busy trying to please others that I end up pleasing no one."

While she was talking, Alice perched on the edge of the chair as if she was a bird about to fall off a branch.

"My jaw aches from being clenched," she admitted. "I'm irritable and edgy. I lose the ability to breathe; it's like my breath gets stuck. I talk fast and my upper back goes into spasms. I feel as though I'm whacked out. I'm not centered or balanced and I get angry with myself for being that way. It's a vicious cycle and I don't see an end in sight."

Alice's story is typical of many people. None of us are immune from the physical effects of stress, but learning to use relaxation exercises can help maintain the sense of balance a body so desperately requires in order to remain healthy. Listen to the cues your body and mind are giving you. Pay close attention to your gut feelings and physical symptoms like sharp pain, twinges, constipation, and trembling eyelids, cheeks and hands. Chronic colds, sinus infections and rashes are a sign that something is out of balance.

Managing Stress by Staying Present

Some people find sitting quietly and doing nothing overwhelming. They cannot just *be*. However, that's the only way to lessen stress. Yes, I know… the kids are screaming, the TV is blaring, the dog needs walking, you're late for a meeting, the laundry is a mile high, dinner is burning, your boss wants everything done yesterday, and I'm telling you to just sit still for a few moments and breathe. The first response I usually hear is: I can't. This is a natural response for the mind. But do you really want to be a slave to your mind for the rest of your life?

Let's face it, you have two choice: Put down the book and allow everyone around you to make you crazy, or find a quiet place and take five minutes for yourself. Trust me, you really have no other option here, so find a quiet spot and do the following mini-meditation.

With techniques like the mini-meditation described below, and on my website, www.stressreduction.com, you can retain your sense of self and operate from the present moment with less tension and anxiety. Remember, one of the major causes of stress is: "What if?" Since the future will unfold in due time (without your choreography) and in a way you can never predict, staying in the present is essential.

RX #2: Here is a mini-meditation. Remain in the NOW. Don't try to second guess what's coming at you in the next five seconds, and stop worrying about the past. Let it go. Be here. Be in the NOW. Gently close your eyes. Now breathe. Watch your breath. Feel your chest expand with each inhale and contract with each exhale. Everything is always perfect in the present moment. Breathe again and relax your shoulders. There's nothing you can do to change the past and the future does not exist in the present.

Shelly's Story – Staying Centered

Fifty years ago you could board a shuttle from Boston to New York without a ticket. Trips across the border were simpler; most people got through customs in a flash. But times have changed, and it's not as simple as it once was to get from point A to point B.

My friend Shelly found this out first-hand. Since she is a Canadian citizen, she would have to go through U.S. Customs and

Immigration before boarding her plane in Buffalo, N.Y. Shelly was singled out and sent to a holding room where she was given a piece of paper with a number.

"A man in a military uniform began to ask me a lot of questions," Shelly told me. "He refused me entry, which took me by complete surprise. His tone was unduly harsh as he fired questions at me. I'm a gentle person by nature and certainly not a terrorist. I didn't have clear answers to his questions and the more he asked the more confused and stressed I became."

"Since this was my first experience coming to America, I was shaking. The officer asked why I was coming to the U.S. and he wanted to make sure I wasn't going to stay here and not return to Canada."

"He asked me for pay stubs or utility bills, which I didn't have. Really, who travels with those things? His attitude was very harsh and I had difficulty thinking beyond his obvious show of anger. I felt myself shutting down."

"I just wanted to get on the plane. By then I realized that this unpleasant encounter had caused me to miss my flight, which added to my stress. My pocketbook was on the counter and he kept asking for verification as to the reason for my trip. I'd already shown him my passport and my driver's permit."

"But he thought I was holding out on him. He kept asking what was in my purse and finally he reached for it. I grabbed it away and showed him there was nothing of interest. But I could feel my blood pressure rising and I wanted to scream. Finally, he let me go. Since I had missed my flight, I had to wait ten more hours for the next one. I went to the ladies' room for a good cry and felt a little better."

When confronted by belligerence or hostility from a stranger, friend or lover, a good cry is one way to diffuse the trauma. When emotions are stirred up and the nervous system stimulates the cranial nerve in the brain, it sends signals from the neurotransmitters to the tear glands, hence the need to cry.

Tears contain chemical proteins and hormones. Scientists have discovered that emotional tears contain high levels of manganese and the hormone prolactin. Crying reduces both of these chemicals in the body and often acts as a calming device because it returns the body to a state of chemical balance.

This next stress reducer ("Rx") may be quite useful:

Rx #3: Crying is an appropriate response when stress becomes unbearable. So when you feel the urge, let it out. Let the tears fly and don't bottle up your stress where it can wreak havoc on your body and make you ill.

Once Shelly was on the plane and settled in her seat, she felt calmer and more in control. Her past trauma, though still raw, seemed far away. After adding a regimen of deep breathing techniques, she arrived in Florida with a smile on her face. In a few days, her traumatic experience was a distant memory.

The thing to remember when someone attacks you with aggressive or hostile behavior is not to take it personally. Abuse of power is often an inappropriate reaction from an unhappy frustrated person. If this happens to you, remember that you are the target of someone else's anger. If you surrender control and stop resisting you will find the situation loses its grip on you and neutralizes in your favor.

The Ripple Effect

Shelly's situation evoked a response known as the "Ripple Effect." Picture a pebble being thrown into a pond. As it sinks, ripples spread toward the shore. Although the stone is gone, the ripples will continue crashing upon the shore.

Like a rock tossed in a pond, nervous energy also creates agitation and irritation. Like the ripples, the nervous energy is projected inward, outward and back toward us – it won't go away until we become conscious of it and release it through awareness.

In Shelly's case she lost control of her thoughts and emotions. Although she felt she was treated unfairly, it was possible for her to change her interpretation – and thoughts – about the event and transform her experience.

You may be wondering: How could Shelly have transformed her thought when the security guard was firing questions at her? How could she have changed her behavior when she realized that she was going to miss her flight?

This is what I told Shelly.

"The world we live in is often turbulent; we don't live on a Planet Fair, we live on Planet Earth. When we accept what is occurring, rather than personalize unpleasant and stressful situations, it will take the "charge" out of the experience. That in turn will neutralize the event. If we choose to see our life as unfolding perfectly in the context of the moment for our benefit, we drop our expectations of needing it to be a certain way. This brings peace.

"But I felt violated," said Shelly.

"Don't take it personally." I told her. "Our society is extremely fear-based. Some people who work in customs, immigration and airport security can be heavy-handed, intimidating, impersonal and downright rude. But their behavior has nothing to do with you. Instead, it is a reflection of their inability to handle the stress in their lives. For you, the opportunity is to have patience and understanding for others and to be in control of your thoughts and reactions.

Shelly nodded, thought a minute and then said: "But what can I do next time?"

"In the Eastern discipline Tai Chi, there is a body movement called ward off and neutralize. If someone comes at you, whether physically or verbally, gently step aside and let their aggressiveness move past you. If you don't resist, there is nothing to attack."

"There was no place for me to step aside." Shelly protested.

"If we remain calm, centered and neutral in an adverse and unpleasant situation we won't absorb the negative energy directed our way," I told her. "Offer no resistance, knowing that this too shall pass, and you will gain a sense of control rather than fear and frustration. In other words: Let go and go with the flow."

Linda's Story – Stand and Fight

"Go with the flow" took on a whole new meaning when Linda awoke to a flood in her new condo. And the worst part is that Linda had recently installed a new hardwood floor. Within minutes she found her kitchen floor covered in water. Immediately her adrenaline began to pump as she grabbed for towels and called a friend for help.

"It was awful," she told me. "The floor was ruined and the water had run into the hallway and dining room. It was devastating: I had to pull up thousands of dollars of brand-new flooring just to throw it away."

"Life happens," I said to Linda when she called in hysterics, "so be proactive. Yes, it's disappointment. But staying upset about something you cannot change is futile; it only causes more distress. Accept it and then take action: Decide what you need to do."

The stress that Shelly and Linda experienced came from two completely different sources, yet the effect was the same. They were anxious, tense, and their adrenaline was pumping. The way they handled those stressful situations was also completely different. While Shelly needed to be still and let the negativity of the airport guard pass her by, Linda had to immediately take charge of the situation, rather than stand around and complain. If she hadn't taken charge, her entire apartment would have been ruined.

There are so many causes of stress and so many ways to handle it. But both Shelly and Linda are examples that illustrate the flight-or-fight dynamics of stress. The best response will be dictated by the situation. Shelly took flight, literally, and it was the correct thing to do in that situation. Linda, on the other hand, had to stand and fight. And that was also correct.

In any tense situation there are certain things you can do to minimize the tension, so let's get to it.

This Game Called Life

Life is a balancing act. You'll have good days and bad days. Your luck can change in a nanosecond. You can win the lottery or be struck by lightning. So the trick is to learn to manage your stress. That means staying in the NOW. Are you in the NOW or are you somewhere else?

Ask yourself the following questions:

> ➤ How often do I wallow in the past, thinking about things that cannot be changed?

> ➤ Do I fret and become upset because I did something I feel I shouldn't?

> ➤ Do I wish that I could change yesterday?

> ➤ Do I wish tomorrow would come sooner – or not at all?

> ➤ Do I cling to old thoughts and feelings for weeks or months at a time?

> ➤ Do I get ahead of myself by projecting myself into the future?

> ➤ Do I rehearse what I will say or do in a certain situation?

> ➤ Do I plan what I'll have for the next meal hours before eating?

If you are like most people, you answered yes to many of the questions above. While a certain amount of planning and goal-setting is important for staying focused, most of us waste too much time daydreaming about situations that will never happen. Even if they do occur, they will likely be different from what we imagined anyway. Meanwhile the present is slipping away quickly, turning into the past, and you are missing out on life.

Past and future are mental concepts; as such they are imaginary, not real. So if you're projecting what should happen or what might happen, you're not only robbing yourself of the NOW, you're also creating thoughts that are likely causing stress. The NOW is the ONLY place to be – because in the NOW, at this very moment, while you're reading these words, everything is OK. You are alive: you are breathing and probably have enough food to eat. The problem is that we tend to get ahead of ourselves and imagine what will happen next. But that usually never happens anyway. And that, my friends, is the beauty of life.

Try to be mindful of what is going on around you at all times. When you're washing dishes, pay attention to what you're doing. Be one with the water and the soap. Accept the fact that the dishes need to be cleaned and that there is a reason for doing it and enjoy the process. Be in the moment instead of wishing you were somewhere else. The moment is much more enjoyable, take my word for it.

Rx #4: Reduce stress by accepting the situations in your life as they are in this moment – and I mean every aspect of them. Stop thinking about what should be happening or who you think you should be.

Betty likes movies. "It's my relaxing time." She told me. "It's a wonderful place to unwind, it's dark and quiet, and usually the movie is entertaining."

But Betty often gets herself in a frenzy trying to accomplish everything on her agenda and ends up not being able to attend the movie. She's certainly not alone. Rushing through life from task to task is our society's dilemma, like a country song – "I'm in a hurry and I don't know why."

Getting ahead of ourselves is as common as an old penny. How often have you thought about what you're having for dinner while you're having breakfast? Or what you'll wear tomorrow or to the party on Saturday? You're drawn into a future that doesn't exist.

What if you have a big lunch and don't want dinner? What if you're stuck in traffic and miss dinner? What if you wake up sick and can't go to work? What if the party is cancelled? So many things can happen that it boggles the mind.

"When I give up the idea of going to the movies, time slows down," says Betty. "I get everything accomplished and I take a twenty-minute nap, which makes me feel far more relaxed than racing to the movie and then having someone next to me talk through it."

Rx #5: SLOW DOWN. When you rush from one thing to the next, you set yourself up for more stress.

All the hustle and bustle of life creates pressure, which in turn makes us more stressed out and ultimately can make us physically ill. So take a deep breath and clear your mind. Now try this mini-relaxation technique.

The Two-minute Breath Exercise

This is a great centering technique for bringing people back to the present moment. If done with awareness it will transport you from the regrets to the past and uncertainty of the future, to the perfect NOW, where everything is in harmony.

Most of us are shallow breathers, and that's especially true during times of stress. To show you what I mean, close your eyes and hold the palm of your hand facing the body. Where are you breathing from? Move your hand to that area. If you're like many people, your hand will be over your chest or throat area.

As we encounter stress in our life we take short shallow breaths. When this happens, we reduce the flow of oxygen throughout the body. It's similar to a light flickering when the plug is not fully inserted in the socket; there is a disconnection. When someone is not grounded through deep breathing, the body needs to be connected to the breath to feel totally secure and happy. This full connection to breath grounds the flow of energy and connects to life.

Sometimes we forget we have a complete electrical system generating a huge amount of energy. When we are not grounded, there is often a feeling of unease accompanied by sensations of light-headedness or an out-of-body feeling.

Resetting Your Thermostat

This simple exercise is like pushing a reset button to rebalance your polarities. It creates an awareness that will bring you back into your body and connect your mind with your body. It is designed to produce a feeling of peace within the body and soul.

This two-minute breath exercise should be done throughout the day – especially when you see your breath is shallow, or when you're feeling anxious, hurried or stressed. It will help you reset your equilibrium.

Are you ready? It's easy and worthwhile – so here we go.

Focus on the lower abdomen, inhale fully through your nose to expand your stomach, and then slowly exhale through your mouth. Now repeat this, and when you exhale the second breath do not force the breath, just let it go, like a sigh of relief. Breathe one more time if you still feel frazzled. Take a deep breath in through your nose, expanding your stomach, and exhale through your mouth.

It's perfectly fine to let out a moan or sigh of delight. By now you are probably experiencing a sense of well-being and calm. If not, keep going until you do. It's pretty amazing what you can accomplish in only a few minutes.

When I do this with a room full of people, the shift in energy is palpable. Once, while giving a talk about stress reduction to doctors and their spouses, I had everyone put down their eating utensils, drinks and cell phones.

"This two minute exercise will benefit you as busy caregivers," I said. "It's important to do this as often as possible because people in the medical profession are said to have a lifespan ten years shorter than the average person."

After everyone finished the breathing exercise, the room was so quiet you could hear an eyelash flutter. Later, several doctors told me that they were amazed how this simple exercise was able to transform them into a serene state.

It is important for you to know that you can move from a place of high anxiety to a place of peace without moving your physical body. It's all about changing the chemistry of your mind and clearing your thoughts through breathing.

Chapter 2

A BELLY FULL OF STRESS

"Nothing in the affairs of men is worthy of great anxiety" – Plato

A Quiz: WHAT DOES FOOD MEAN TO YOU?

If you are what you eat, then what should you eat? The right answer is healthy food. Healthy food makes you feel good about yourself. While junk food may calm your nerves temporarily, it might cause you extreme anxiety and even depression when you can't zip up your pants or ties your shoes.

Stress tends to bring out the worst in our eating habits. To help you assess your relationship between stress and the food you eat, take a moment to answer the following questions. Remember, be honest with yourself – it's critical if you want to change things.

1. Is your weight relative to your height?

Yes or No

2. Do you lack awareness and control of your physical well-being?

Yes or No

3. Do you ignore the nutritional value of what you eat?

Yes or No

4. Do you eat when you're sad, lonely or angry?

Yes or No

5. Do you treat food as a substitute for love and affection?

Yes or No

6. Do you eat whether or not you are hungry?

Yes or No

7. Do you think about food all day?

Yes or No

8. Do you feel guilty about eating?

Yes or No

9. Do you chew fast and swallow without tasting it?

Yes or No

10. Is some form of cardiac exercise (walking briskly or cycling) at least 30-45 minutes five days weekly missing from your life?

Yes or No

If you answered no to at least half of these questions, you are being mindful about food and taking care of your body – that's a good thing. If you answered yes to more than three of these questions, you probably have an issue with food and caring for your body in a healthy way. At the very least, you might be lacking healthy weight-control habits and sooner or later these habits will catch up with you.

If you answered yes to more than half of the questions, you are a prime candidate for developing future health problems. So commit now to physical health and well being. Professionals such as nutritionists, exercise physiologists, chiropractors, physical therapists, personal trainers and some physicians can assist you in overcoming eating disorders and teach you how to care for your body through exercise and healthy food choices. Consult them before starting a new exercise or eating program.

A Belly Full of Stress

Stand outside a movie theater or mall and take a look at the people who walk by. Most jiggle as they walk because they are overweight. It is a conservative estimate that six out of ten people are overweight. Experts predict that at the rate we're going, 75 percent of all Americans will be obese by the year 2015! It's easy to blame the U.S. government, fast food restaurants, MSG, radio waves, the internet and cell phones. But ultimately, stress is the culprit and your challenge is to overcome it.

Stress and food are likely companions. Those who use food as a crutch when they feel out of control end up catching the "juggle effect." We're often bombarded by demands from work, relationships, children, goals and expectations (self-imposed or from others). We have so many balls in the air that when one drops we need to console ourselves.

That's why we crave comfort foods, which are rich in calories, sugar or starch. The result is an expanding torso or a ballooning behind. But the object of our affection – food – doesn't alleviate our anxiety at all. Instead, we develop a belly full of stress.

Breaking the Emotional Eating Cycle

Food is such an emotionally charged issue that it can become the ultimate stress inducer. Stress – more than any other emotional issue leads to overeating. The pressure could be from not losing enough weight, tension at work, a relationship (or lack of one), financial problems, boredom, increased responsibilities, clinging to the past or an insatiable appetite for wanting something you don't have. When we are unable to handle the tension and emotions created by life's events, many of us turn to food for relief.

Some people accept the extra pounds because they don't want to fix the problem that led them to overeat. This can come from deep-seated childhood traumas that turned their life upside down. For example, it is not uncommon for women who have been molested to gain weight. It's a well known self-protective mechanism clinically referred to as "stuffing the emotions."

There's an expression that fat people are happy people. But I can vouch from experience as a therapist that this is a myth. CNN.com recently profiled a married couple who were a classic example of an unhappy overweight pair. Maggie Sorrells and her husband, Andy, tipped the scales at a combined weight of nearly 1,000 pounds! At age 27, Maggie weighed an astonishing 400 pounds and Andy, who was in his late twenties, had ballooned to 500. Although Maggie had been warned by doctors that she wouldn't live to celebrate her 30th birthday, she continued with her emotional overeating. "I was the funny fat girl, but inside I wasn't laughing; I was miserable." She recalls.

Andy was teased mercilessly and eventually withdrew and turned to anti-depressants. The couple from Franklin, Tennessee, met online and continued their binging until one day they made a commitment to The Weigh-Down Workshop, a faith-based weight loss program that teaches people to conquer food addiction by turning toward God for support.

By the time they were profiled on the internet, Andy had lost 220 pounds and Maggie 300 for an incredible total loss of 520 pounds. They could barely recognize themselves. They were ecstatic and admitted that they had no idea life could be so good.

Emotional eating is a vicious cycle. Unhappiness, anxiety, trauma, and nervous tension can lead to serial eating or constant snacking on junk food. That leads to weight gain and emotional distress. And no one likes that.

People also overeat when they're feeling good. Emotions can create excitement that is sometimes uncomfortable. Newlyweds are known to gain ten pounds in the first year of marriage when they're deliriously in love, but also dealing with the stress of starting a new life.

Tea (and more) for Two

Couples who have lived together before marriage often find that after they've tied the knot the dynamics change. And, as many of you know, any significant change can (and often does) cause stress. Like a new pair of shoes, new relationship paradigms need getting used to – they need to be stretched and toned to fit. That "Until death do us part" just might set off a hidden alarm system in your past (or your partner's). Not only that – if you remember the first quiz in this book – you will remember that marriage is one of the top stress agents in this obstacle course of life.

We have found that some married couples no longer feel the need to keep up their physical standard of excellence. The need to be alluring is no longer the motivating force since they've found their ideal match. If you've caught the big fish, do you need to hold onto the bait? The answer depends on your priorities and commitments.

Some spouses feel that once they have found love and happiness, it's OK to let themselves go. In this case, the commitment was to find a mate, not good physical health. Others, however, are committed to maintaining physical health for life simply because they know and understand the benefits. Where do you stand?

Ultimately, we must come to terms with the truth. Perhaps that is why so many fad diets make the cash registers (and the creators) so rich. Everyone's looking for a fast fix, a magic pill, or a brilliant therapist to hypnotize them so they can peel off the pounds. (Maybe even a surgeon to lighten the load.)

How many times have you vowed to go on a diet and given yourself a goal of losing 50 pounds in three months? One month goes by and you've only lost five pounds so you become discouraged. The next thing you know you're buying a gallon of ice cream and eating it in one sitting.

If this sounds familiar, it's not a hopeless situation. But there is a better way. You don't need a magic pill or even an exercise machine. All you need is YOU. You are the magic bullet. Focus on the process and not just the goal, put a plan in place, and get help from others. If your goal is to lose 50 pounds, then ask a trained professional what is a reasonable amount of weight to expect to lose and in what time frame. Learn to be happy with your progress and with losing weight in small increments. Remember, your body was not built in a day, so why would you think you could lose 50 pounds in 30 days?

The real accomplishment would be losing five pounds in three weeks and keeping it off. After that you can set another realistic goal. People often set unrealistic goals and then fail. If you find yourself failing every time you set out to lose weight, consider that you might be trying to climb a mountain without the proper gear (what your body and mind is ready for). When you hit a plateau, which always happens in the weight-loss process, don't become discouraged and return to the old habits that put the pounds on in the first place. Instead, be prepared and get the support you need to work through the adjustment period.

Unfortunately, dieting often does more harm than good. Food deprivation makes the body fight back by wanting to store food (as fat) as a hedge against future starvation. Let's face it, the body needs food to survive and it will tell you when it needs to be fed. If you listen carefully, you will know what your body wants. If this sounds like clairvoyance, it is in a way. You and your body are one. You are both part of the same spirit, the same motivating desire to be healthy and happy. But beware: A healthy body does not crave food. If you are craving junk food it means that your body is out of balance and not receiving the nutrition that it needs. Similarly, pills that quench the appetite do a disservice because they mask the body's need for nourishment.

You must realize that you didn't gain all those extra pounds in a week or a month or even a year. It takes time to put weight on and time to take it off. Putting pressure on yourself to fit into a certain size by a certain date only adds stress. And the outcome is almost always disastrous.

And you know what happens? You end up on that rollercoaster of gaining and losing, losing and gaining, that's sometimes called the yo-yo diet. Oprah Winfrey often goes through this battle of the bulge, but the difficult thing for her is that she has to do it in front of millions of people. You are luckier – you don't have a national audience!

Do you remember when Oprah pulled a wagon of 60 pounds of fat on stage? She was thin as a rail at that time, but over the years her weight has fluctuated wildly. The stress of running a multi-billion-dollar conglomerate ends up on her hips and thighs, even though she has access to the best food, the best chefs and the best personal trainers. Oprah is honest with herself and others; she admits to being a stress-motivated overeater. But she keeps working on it. This is what makes such great success possible for her.

Dieting to the End

Yo-yo dieting can lead to binging, purging or anorexia – three potentially deadly diseases. This is especially common with teenagers and college students who feel pressure to keep up with young Hollywood starlets who starve themselves. It doesn't look pretty to most of us and it's downright dangerous. Many campuses now offer free counseling for students with eating disorders.

If you are a student, get help; if you are a parent with a son or daughter caught in this deadly cycle, find out where help is available. Anyone with the habit of binging and purging should seek the advice of an eating disorder clinic or specialist.

There is only one way to gain control over your eating habits, and it takes willpower. You have to decide to take charge of your life. The problem is that many people don't know how to parent themselves and say no. One of my clients told me about her sister-in-law. "Her stomach keeps saying yes to food and many other things in life. She lives large and is large from taking in too much. And if you get in her way by the buffet, watch out! She'll shove people aside to get to the food."

In this case, her sister-in-law is not only taking in more stress than she can handle but also more food than she needs. Using food as a tranquilizer is a dead-end street, literally.

Being overweight or morbidly obese, which is 100 pounds or more over the national guidelines for height and body frame, is like playing Russian roulette with all the chambers loaded. You may think it's simply about shopping at plus-size stores or being inconvenienced by small airplane seats, but it's much more than that. Obesity leads to a multitude of ailments including heart disease, increased blood pressure, stroke, and type 2 diabetes – the leading cause of amputations and blindness today, which once generally began in adulthood but is now rampant in children.

Type 2 diabetes is an epidemic today, affecting the young as well as middle-aged and older adults. This condition is due to increased weight gain brought on by the failure to exercise and eat sensibly. Type 2 diabetes occurs when the body's cells cannot properly absorb insulin because of excess fat; this causes blood glucose levels to remain dangerously high.

Millions of people with type 2 diabetes – or pre-diabetes – do not know they have it. But it is a serious condition that can lead to kidney disease, eye disease, blindness, nervous system disorder, and loss of circulation, which can lead to amputation. People with diabetes are prone to foot problems because of the likelihood of damage to blood vessels, nerves and a decreased ability to fight infection. Problems with blood flow and damage to nerves may cause an injury to the foot as well as infection. Death of skin and other tissue can occur.

If you are overweight or suspect a diabetic condition, see your physician for a blood test. Additionally, meet with professionals who can assist you with a proper nutrition and exercise program. The good news is that most cases of type 2 diabetes can be completely reversed – eliminating the need for insulin completely – with proper nutrition and exercise. Some people have accomplished this in as little as three weeks with medical supervision.

Rx #6: With eating disorders, as with any recovery process, there must be a lifestyle change. And only YOU can make that change.

As I mentioned at the beginning of this chapter, there's a saying that goes, "you are what you eat." If you're filling up on fast food with little nutritional value – or food that is high in calories and fat – you will not feel good about yourself. You also won't have the energy you need to get through the day. The more weight you gain, the unhappier you may become. As your waistline expands your wallet will shrink, because you will have to invest in a new wardrobe. Then there is the added cost of increased doctor's visits and medication, not to mention extra food.

The stress of spending will add to your financial worries and detract from your sense of self-worth, creating even more worries and anxiety. Doesn't it make better sense to learn how to deal with the stresses in life now before they become threatening to your physical health?

Brad's Story – Eating as Meditation

Brad, a 35-year-old bachelor, weighed more than 300 pounds when he came to see me. He loved to eat and drink and quipped that "water is for bathing, not drinking." A writer with a sedentary lifestyle, Brad thought exercising was for wimps, although he huffed and puffed as he walked toward the store on his never-ending quest for food. He had never had a serious relationship and admitted he found eating more satisfying than sex. Although his doctor had warned him that there were inevitable and dire consequences to his eating disorder and subsequent obesity, Brad turned a deaf ear.

"My parents were fat, my brothers were fat and I'm fat," he told me. "I inherited it.

As I watched his face turn beet read and his jowls shake as he spoke, I wondered if he really thought he could blame his current physical state on his parents. Brad was like many other obese people, blaming their genes for tipping the scales. Yet studies show less than three percent of overweight people have a genetic predisposition. It's a simple equation: Children eat what – and how – their parents eat. Therefore, many children become clones of their parents, embracing and emulating the lifestyle they saw growing up even if it means becoming morbidly obese.

Brad was intelligent and he wanted to lose weight. Yet, in his subconscious mind, he didn't believe weight loss was possible because of his family history. Brad had no sense of personal responsibility. Because his family was fat and had suffered the plight of serious problems like strokes, heart attacks, and complications from diabetes, he couldn't' shake off his fat self-image.

"I can't lose weight," he told me numerous times during our ongoing sessions. "I joined a gym and got a personal trainer. I lost six pounds in three months and then gained it back."

"Did you change your eating habits?" I asked. "Not really," he replied. "That could be part of it, but it also could be that you don't believe that you can lose the weight." I said. "You took some positive steps, lost some weight, but gained it back. Somewhere inside you just don't believe it's possible. There is no magic bullet. What you need is to reduce the quantity of food you eat, adopt a regular exercise program and shift your underlying beliefs. Perhaps you should try hypnotherapy."

Brad did not warm up to the idea of hypnotherapy right away, so I told him a story about a boy and a cookie.

"Like most kids, we like chocolate chip cookies. Growing up, this boy's parents doled out one cookie at a time rather than allowing him to devour the entire bag. Their philosophy was more is NOT better.

"The child would hold the cookie in anticipation of its delectable taste. Savoring this sacrament, he'd look at it from every angle, and ultimately he took a small bite and reveled in its journey to his stomach."

"Sometimes he would take 10 to 15 minutes to relish in this occasion. This is joyous eating. If everything we put in our mouths and swallowed was done with the same reverence we wouldn't be the world's fattest society."

Brad nodded. I think he "got it." So I continued.

"The Eater's Rule is to drink what you chew and chew what you drink," I told him. "Take small bites and chew each mouthful 30 times; put down the fork in between bites. This not only results in the full release of digestive enzymes but also reduces the quantity of food eaten."

I explained that eating can become a form of mindful meditation. The joy comes from being appreciative of the food that makes your body the wonderful machine it is. Rather than mindlessly devouring a bag of cookies, each bite should become a reflection of your good fortune. When done in silence you can focus on that joy. This is what being mindful about food is about.

As Brad found out, it's difficult to change a lifelong pattern that affects us negatively. We're told to do this or do that. Nobody says: "Just be who you are."

However, if you can sit quietly and watch your thoughts as they arise, you will discover what food represents to you. If you listen to your body without letting your mind wander to thoughts of juicy hamburgers or pizza with extra cheese, you will anchor yourself in the present moment. You will be grounded and food will become less important.

Brad listened attentively and took my advice. He agreed to hypnotherapy and nutritional education. Brad made a rapid and exhilarating transformation. He went from fat and unhappy to in-shape and inspired.

Rx #7: You and only YOU are responsible for your own well-being. Only YOU can make yourself sick or well, heavy or slender. It's all up to you. Only YOU can take responsibility for your own actions. No one is forcing you to overeat – you made that decision and that means you have the power to reverse that decision.

Rushing all the Way

Let's take a closer look at the dynamics. Remember we are only human. Sometimes we make poor choices: we eat too much, we eat the wrong foods, we do things we know we shouldn't. And then we feel bad about ourselves. We say, "If I can't be perfect, I won't even try." In essence, we punish ourselves for making bad decisions.

For example, you rush to make a plane, you miss it, and you beat yourself up because you missed an important meeting. What do you do next? Go to the food court and order a double cheeseburger and a huge plate of fries. You start shoveling food into your mouth out of frustration. And that's the wrong reason for eating.

There is a lesson to learn here: Stop being so hard on yourself. We are only human, and human beings make mistakes. Your choices give you chance to become a better you. Learn from your actions and learn to accept and forgive yourself, just as you might forgive someone else who made a mistake.

Consider the example of Francine, a single woman in her early forties who was grossly overweight. Her self-esteem was low and she had trouble coping with her coworkers. She was also burdened by an alcoholic mother and an elderly father who needed surgery.

"My father is pressuring me to move home," she told me. "That's a major source of anxiety. But I worry even more about not having enough money. And, above all, I want to lose weight."

Francine admitted that when she felt stressed she turned to chocolate. "It makes me feel better," she said. "I derive tremendous satisfaction from eating a hot fudge sundae. But afterwards I feel guilty."

During our sessions, I realized that Francine was enveloped by dark moods. She lived in a small, cluttered apartment and felt as though nobody cared. She was living one continuous pity party, which was compounded by her expanding weight.

"I'd like to lose one hundred pounds," she admitted. "And it kills me because my mother and sister are both petite." In fact, Francine's top weight was almost 250 pounds, and although she had joined numerous weight-loss programs she'd always regained the weight she had lost.

In addition to the stress about her weight, Francine had never married; she felt added pressure to find the perfect mate. Instead of going out to find love she wallowed in anxiety and fear about every aspect of her life.

"I feel like I'm a happy person somewhere inside, but I can't deal with all the stress," she said. "I need help."

Everyone wants to feel good and not be filled with apprehension. Yet most of us are in a box that makes us feel trapped. Francine was trapped in the self-pity box.

We talked about giving up chocolate for five days. "It's like taking a baby step," I told her, "By making this decision and sticking to it you will be empowering yourself. And if you add a half-hour of walking a day, not only will you have more energy, your self-esteem will rise because endorphins – the happy hormones – are released."

We also discussed uncluttering her apartment. Francine agreed to hire a cleaning person for a one-time cleaning. "It changed my life," she later told me cheerfully. "I feel as though I'm in control of my life and that means I can take control of my eating. It seems like such a simple thing, I don't know why I didn't think of it before."

Within six months, Francine left her low-paying job and was making more money. She also had begun to lose weight and was on the right path to gaining her sense of self. She didn't let her father pull her into his net of neediness by moving back home. Instead, she offered to help pay for the cost of a home-care professional.

"I've learned to say no, and it's a wonderful feeling," she told me at one of our last sessions. "I'm no longer using food to make me happy; instead I go walking four times a week and on days I can't go, I miss it. I'm also eating smaller portions and enjoying them more."

Rx #8: For every concept that holds you back – beating yourself up for past mistakes is a big one – there is a recipe for true healing: Relax into the present moment and leave the past behind.

Julio, a middle aged businessman, is an example of this. When he came to see me he was depressed and suicidal. The reason: He had suffered a stroke and a heart attack. He had three stents in his heart and 80 percent blockage in his arteries. But even worse, Julio's frustration had reached epidemic proportions. He ranted that he felt cheated by life.

"Sure, I'm alive," he said, "but I'll be sad for the rest of my life."

"Why are you here?" I asked.

"I want to walk again without a cane and I want to use my right arm again. Since my stroke, it's been useless."

"I'm not a miracle worker," I told him. "But, I do have some tools that may help you if you would like. The first one is: You must accept where you are now and not cling to the past. Your life now is what you must embrace. The past is gone, the future is uncertain, and you only have the NOW.

Julio was obviously stuck in the past. He avoided the present because he did not like what was happening to him in the now. Julio was so unhappy with his current situation that his only comfort was to cling to the past. Many of us do that. We feel like hostages held against our will by something outside ourselves that we cannot control. It can be emotional (the loss of a loved one) or physical (a serious medical problem). Because we detest the present moment, we are not willing to see what good it has to offer.

If we knew that every seemingly bad event or condition comes with hidden gifts (learning "being" the most important), then perhaps we could embrace the present as a "present". The very site of pain is often the exact spot that holds pleasure – if you can accept it. Being angry with the cards you are dealt does nothing to make your current situation any better. Like a child who spills milk on the floor and ignores what is on his plate, we end up filled with remorse instead of embracing the joy that might be surrounding us. Trust me; there are gifts all around us. You just have to see them.

Often a horrendous experience can teach the biggest lesson and bring the most joy. Self-growth is ultimately why we are here. (Sorry – I wish I had better news). But you don't want to be stuck on an airplane circling above the clouds, do you? Well, then why would you want to stay exactly as you are indefinitely? The trick is to enjoy the growth.

I know it sounds crazy, but it is the truth. If you knew that you were going to school to learn a new subject, would you feel badly if you failed a course? Of course you would. But in the end – after repeating it – you would learn the material and go on to become a better student, right?

Well, consider life as one big course in Earth school. You came to learn, and in the earth school you might get some tough course work. Like everything in life, there are the easier times (love, friendship and a hot fudge sundae) and more difficult times (physical illness or the loss of a loved one). Is your life designed to teach you something? You bet it is. The key is to see the beauty in all of it.

Now back to Julio. During the course of our sessions, I learned that Julio's diet consisted of chicken salad sandwiches with extra mayonnaise; bologna sandwiches on white bread; rice and pork; Hot Pockets with egg, cheese and bacon; pork chops; canned potatoes and fast food. Julio didn't cook and never ate salads, fruit or green vegetables.

He continually moaned about "what I used to have and how I used to be." Stuck in his misery, Julio refused to get involved in social activities. Instead he focused on what he could not do. He berated the doctors and assured himself and others that they were giving him poor advice. "What did they know?" He said bitterly.

"I want to go for a walk," he often told me. "But I can't walk and I'll have to accept it – I just don't want to."

Like many people who experience things in life they cannot change, Julio blamed everyone but himself. Yet, it was Julio's doing that had undone him. It was his terrible eating habits and choice of foods that caused his health problems. But "poor me" does little in the way of healing these days. It does keep a lot of therapists in business, however.

Julio completed my stress reduction program and complained every step of the way. But his blood pressure dropped and so did his cholesterol. Ultimately he proved to himself that he had the ability to change his ways. He made new friends, despite his depression, and established contacts with others. The interesting thing is that he found friends who had even bigger problems than he did – some with terminal illnesses.

You could say that letting go of the past gave Julio a new present. He has more hope and is helping his progress and his prognosis. He has acupuncture weekly, attends stroke support classes, and has become an avid reader of health books. He also attends meditation retreats (which I recommend to anyone, healthy or otherwise).

"I feel more focused on what I have and less focused on what I don't have," he told me recently. "I'm making healthier choices. I'm living more in the now and not as much in the past. I can't change what has happened to me; I can only go forward to make my life better."

Anna's Story – Escaping Through Food

Anna came to see me after having gained 75 pounds in just over one year. After raising 12 children, she was experiencing "empty nest syndrome." Her husband was deceased and she lived alone. At age 65, she was shocked to see how much flab was hanging from her slender frame.

"I don't understand why I've gained so much weight," she said. "I skip breakfast and usually eat a small salad for lunch."

What Anna didn't mention was that when at the end of her day she yanked open the refrigerator door and kept it open practically all evening. She would devour a gallon of ice cream and eat whatever else was there.

Like so many overweight people who eat because of depression, social habit, addiction, self-loathing, anxiety or boredom, Anna was "stuffing" her emotions. Her life had been devoted to raising a large family, and now that her husband and children were gone the refrigerator had become her way of coping with grief. You could say she was filling her void with food.

After she realized that food had become her substitute family – and her crutch – Anna decided to change her ways. She started working part-time selling clothing. She also became a water connoisseur, consuming the recommended daily requirement (one ounce per one-half of her body weight) to flush out adipose tissue (fat cells) and hydrate her body. Anna stopped buying ice cream so she wouldn't be tempted to indulge her loneliness at night and within three weeks she had dropped twelve pounds.

"I'm beginning to enjoy my new life," she told me. "I feel as though I'm turning back into the old me – the one I used to like."

Maria's Story – The Art of Sabotage

Maria's weight gain started after her 56-year-old husband died unexpectedly of a heart attack just a few weeks after her father passed away. Maria was a 50-year-old workaholic who lived on diet sodas and salads drenched in salad dressing. Like Anna, she was mystified as to why she was packing on pounds, even though she ate so little.

To make matters worse, Maria gained more weight after getting involved in a relationship with a dominating man who moved in with her and seldom worked, but who borrowed money from her to feed his gambling habit.

When she first came to see me, Maria was depressed, 120 pounds overweight, and filled with self-loathing.

"I've been diagnosed with diabetes," she told me. "I hate myself. I won't look in the mirror. I don't own a bathing suit even though I was on the swim team in high school. I have difficulty sleeping and I'm frightened because I have heart palpitations. I don't know what to do."

Maria was no longer exercising and was feeling an enormous amount of stress from her live-in boyfriend, Richard, who was pressuring her to marry him even though they'd only known each other for a few months. Maria met with me in secret so Richard wouldn't know about it. I began teaching Maria how to meditate and encouraged her to add healthier foods to her diet. After a few weeks, she started exercising and began to regain her self-confidence.

"I feel so much better about myself, I've decided to break it off with Richard," she proudly announced at one of our sessions. "I can't allow him to control me any longer. I'm worth more than that."

I was very pleased with her progress, so it was quite disturbing when Maria failed to show up for her next appointment. I phoned her office and was told she was unable to speak to me. Several days passed before Maria called with an excuse to cancel another appointment.

After a number of tries at contacting her, I learned that Richard had discovered her source of renewed strength when he had overheard her telling a friend about our counseling sessions together. Apparently he felt threatened by her desire to make changes in her life and adamantly forbade her to continue therapy with me. Drained and depressed, she gave in to his demands.

Sometimes people stay in situations that are unhealthy when they become aware of their fears about the alternatives. In Maria's case it was probably her concern about the amount of effort it would take to split from Richard, combined with her fear of being alone, that prevented her from moving forward.

Co-dependant relationships like Maria's are one of the most common causes of uncontrollable eating. Self-sabotage takes many forms and choosing to be in a relationship with someone who supports your weaknesses rather than your strengths is one way of self-sabotage. Rather than getting support, Maria used her relationship as another reason for feeding her emotional void with food. Unless an individual is willing to take personal responsibility for his or her life, change cannot and will not occur. There is no mystery here.

In this case and in other situations like Maria's, the best you can do is to simply acknowledge the fears that have prevented you from moving forward and accept them as a temporary limitation. This act of compassion will bring more peace in the current situation and allow you to move forward.

Rx #9: Making a decision and sticking to it will empower you to reach your goals. There is nothing the human mind cannot accomplish, provided there is the drive or willpower. And the better you feel, the more you will accomplish.

Dropping Expectations

As your levels of expectation rise, so does your stress in trying to achieve them, which often causes failure. When you're overloaded with expectations it is difficult to deal with even the smallest inconvenience. A confrontation at work can end in an eating binge at home. A traffic jam can lead to an angry outburst. But if you can change the expectations that keep you running on the treadmill, you will experience an awakening – or a permanent shift in your way of being in the world.

A good example of this occurred with my next patient, Vicky, a production manager for a national magazine. She was very good at her job and had been with the same company for 15 years. Vicky was also happily married, but she loved to eat. She enjoyed indulging in rich sauces and lots of butter on her food. Of course the downside is that her waistline expanded significantly. Her husband didn't seem to mind, and neither did she. Life was good for Vicky. She was content in her job and in her marriage. She had very little stress in her life until she was fired because of a company downsizing.

Vicky was smart and resilient enough to begin the interview process immediately. But she was worried about presenting the right image. "They'll see me as a fat middle-aged woman," she told me. "Who'd want to hire me?"

So Vicky said goodbye to butter and cream sauces and enrolled in yoga and Pilates classes. Slimmer and more confident, she was immediately hired by a local newspaper. She might have been hired anyway, but being fired was the wake-up call Vicky needed to make a much-needed change in her life. She shifted her energy from mindless eating to being conscious about her calorie and fat intake.

Vicky also did another key thing – she started an exercise program. That in turn, caused her mental attitude to change 180 degrees. In the end, Vicky felt 100 percent better about herself. She substituted exercise for food as a way of feeding her emotional and spiritual being.

Think of your progress as a work in progress. You work on different pieces of your life and put them together as if you were working on a building or writing a book. You start with one piece, one action or one sentence, and build from there.

That's what happened to me when I met Elvis. Yes, the real Elvis Presley. I met the king of rock 'n' roll when my family moved to Memphis, Tennessee. It turned out that Presley lived right down the street from us. That was a big deal to a young fellow from Columbia, South Carolina. But I didn't let it erode my expectations or spoil my excitement about meeting this legendary singing icon.

Instead of thinking negatively or having unrealistic expectations, like adults sometime do, my brother and I simply knocked on his front door. Then we did what came naturally – we asked to see Elvis, sure that our request would be met. And that's exactly what happened.

The maid who answered the door said, "Mister Elvis is out back." As we walked past the pink Cadillac in the carport we saw Elvis sitting on the patio in a purple shirt, white pants and suede shoes. As we walked toward Elvis, a woman was dusting dirt from Elvis's car into an envelope.

Despite all the fanfare and posturing, Elvis was a cool guy. The next time we went to his house, Elvis was driving up with a pretty blonde. But he still found time to get out of the car and pose for pictures in the driveway with my brother Les and me.

The sad part of the story is that Elvis did not have a happy life. No amount of adoration or money could eliminate his stress and painful thoughts. The icon of the ages couldn't let the good times roll; he had expectations from life (and from others) that were always unrequited. Perhaps he thought that life would take care of him if he had more money and more cars, but it never did. Instead it just proved to be a filter that allowed this insulated man of despair to falter.

If it wasn't for his cars and money (and the yes-men), Elvis might have found the help he needed. Instead he fell through the cracks of sanity and wellness by not having to look at his stress levels or his pain.

But to me, Elvis is an integral part of my life. I still remember him wrapping his arms around Les and me. We took a whole sequence of photos, not only of Elvis but his house and lawn too, and when we got back to South Carolina, we were like rock stars. Girls swooned as they passed around our Elvis photos like gold bullion.

Rx #10: Change is difficult. So make ONE behavioral correction each day and do not worry about tomorrow. You know why – because tomorrow always takes care of itself.

Mindful eating – Think…Think…Think About What You Eat

Most people eat on automatic pilot. They have a short lunch break so they grab what's handy from a fast food joint, scoff it down and swallow, barely chewing. Or, they go to the vending machine for chips and soda and call it a meal. It is amazing how many people pick up fast food for dinner and eat it in front of the television. This is often called unconscious eating because it's done mechanically without thought. This way of eating often occurs when emotions are suppressed or repressed.

Once unconscious eating becomes habitual, your biological hunger clock no longer does its job. Instead of letting our bodies tell us when we're ready to eat, we override the urge and go on automatic pilot. When this happens we are no longer in sync with one of nature's most valuable gifts – our biological magnificence. The worst part of automatic pilot is that the people who do this are never really satisfied because their hunger isn't physical but emotional.

The only way to break this negative food state is to face it, deal with it and make a commitment to be mindful about what you eat and when you eat. It is critical to separate emotional eating from the act of nourishing oneself.

Back to Brad

You may recall Brad's overeating story a little earlier. His road to weight recovery started with one cookie. With Brad, the use of a simple exercise using a cookie was the key to understanding. As he sat across from me in my office, I opened my desk drawer, pulled out a bag of chocolate chip cookies, and offered him one.

"Rather than devouring the whole bag of cookies, each bite should bring a reflection," I said. "This way you can focus on the joy of the cookie. It's called being mindful when you eat."

Brad was quiet and neither of us spoke for a minute. I could almost hear his mental activity and sense that his past conditioning was coming to the forefront of consciousness. When he finally broke the silence, Brad's eyes were moist. "I wish my parents had the wisdom to allow me only one cookie," he said.

Each of us ate just one cookie. We took our time and savored each bite. It took a full 15 minutes.

"That was the best damn cookie I've had in my whole life," he said.

Brad's story is one that exemplifies the successful outcome that anyone can have if they learn to pay attention to their body. If you are willing to keep an open mind and accept change then you will undoubtedly see results.

Brad also agreed to start hypnotherapy sessions, which helped him understand more about the destructive tendencies that led to his obesity. With that enlightenment, he embarked on a journey determined to change his life. By working with his marketing strategies think-tank group, Brad was able to create a weight-loss program specifically for him. People like Brad often cling to the past and blame their weight problems on everyone else instead of taking responsibility for themselves.

Brad also sought out a support system, which is advisable (why else would groups such as Weight Watchers make billions of dollars each year?). He found participants by putting the word out in a weekly newspaper column. The results were far more than he anticipated. When the group gathered, not only did they share their personal stories, they helped to promote each others' well being. Within two years, Brad lost 68 pounds, regained his self-esteem, and completely changed his lifestyle to reflect what his goal was — to be healthy and happy.

Rx #11: Unless you are willing to take responsibility for your life (all of it) you will continue to be stuck where you are now. If you want to change the outcome you must change what is happening inside of you. That means being diligent about the life choices you make, the relationships you encounter, the food you eat and the exercise you do (or don't do). If you don't do that, you will remain stuck where you are. If your intent is to lose weight, then you must eat mindfully.

So, you might be thinking, how do I eat mindfully? First and foremost, eat only when you are hungry. If you eat for other reasons check your motivation. Are you frustrated, depressed, lonely, angry, frightened or anxious? Look at the previous questions on food. Are you using food to avoid dealing with challenging emotions?

When you find yourself thinking "I want to eat but I'm not hungry," take a pause. Look into your heart (that is where the emotional circuit-breakers are) and ask: What am I really feeling? Then instead of eating your pain away, allow yourself to feel what you are feeling. It is OK to cry, it is OK to take your tennis racquet and hit balls against the wall, it is OK to just sit quietly and reflect on what you are feeling. These exercises may take time, but they are calorie-free. And the emotional release is so cleansing you will feel like you have eaten a piece of double fudge cake.

You will notice that once you stop your emotional eating binges your body will tell you what it wants and when. The innate wisdom of our body is all-knowing – it will tell you what vitamins, minerals, and enzymes it needs at all times. And that usually means everything should be taken in moderation. Be aware of what you're putting into your mouth. Read labels at the supermarket to make sure what is in the food you eat.

For instance, you might think that all cereals are alike, but that's not true. Check the portion size and then check the calorie count, sugar and fat content. If a half cup of granola has 240 calories and one cup of Special K has 100 calories, it's a no brainer: eat the Special K. Although granola might contain healthy oats and more bran, one cup of it with milk has more than 600 calories. There are better options, so check websites of reputable nutritionists to expand your food repertoire, or visit my site, www.stressreduction.com.

Food for Thought – Low Cal Common Sense

A handful of potato chips have the same number of calories as ten cups of popcorn! Two slices of cheese pizza have twice as many calories as two cups of minestrone soup and a salad with tomatoes and artichoke hearts. A small Caesar salad with chicken, dressing and croutons has as many calories as a hamburger fully loaded. So don't think you're going to slim down eating salad if it's drenched in dressing. It is important to read the label on the back of your salad dressing to see how many calories and fat one tablespoon contains. I think you'll be surprised to find out that your salad dressing may be putting inches on your waist. Now think of all the tablespoons of dressing you've been putting on those so-called healthy salads.

Rx 12: You wouldn't buy a house or a car without knowing the price. So why would you put food in your mouth without knowing what it is going to cost you in calories and potential extra weight?

Once you are in tune with your body, you'll start to notice that certain foods turn you on more than others. Chances are they won't be the sweet, fattening ones; they'll be produce and fresh fruit. These foods will make you body hum. "Hum" foods are what the body desires and requires when you are genuinely hungry. Walk slowly, from aisle to aisle; listen to what your body wants. If you end up with a cart full of pastries, ice cream and fattening foods get another cart and start over. Food that's good for you makes your body run like a Mercedes Benz, not an old clunker.

Look at healthy cookbooks and make a shopping list of things to make those dishes. It's less expensive to eat a healthy low-fat diet if you stick to the produce section and the bulk-food section. Avoid the aisles where you will be tempted to purchase prepackaged and processed foods. These foods are much more expensive and not nearly as nutritious. You'll not only shrink the cost of your grocery bill, you'll shrink your waistline.

Whole grains and fresh vegetables are the way to go. And for people who say they don't have time to eat this way, here's the good news. Cooking with fresh vegetables and grains is simple. The preparation is easy and it will make you fit and healthy. It's a win-win situation all around.

Rx #13: Pay attention to what your body needs and fuel up with healthful food, not junk food.

A Belly Full of Laughs

All of us want to be happy. We want to be comfortable, healthy, financially secure, clothed, fed, sheltered and loved – not necessarily in that order. When one of these ingredients is missing we feel stressed. By definition, stress is "a state of intense strain: constraining force or influence, activity, or exertion for the accomplishment of anything." Stress is part of the human condition and nobody is immune. No matter how rich, poor or healthy you might be, stress will always lurk in the shadows. That is why it is important to know how to deal with it and keep it to a minimum.

The antidote to stress is relaxation. It is impossible to be both stressed out and relaxed at the same time. When we are relaxed we are content. And when are content we are calm and at peace. Life is good and food is not something we rely on to fill us up or make us happy.

Being overweight is not pleasant. Think of every 10 pounds as a bowling ball. If you carried two bowling balls around all day, every day, everywhere you went and couldn't put them down for even a second, you would be exhausted. And that's only 20 pounds! If you are 50, 80 or 120 pounds overweight, that's the equivalent of five, eight or more bowling balls that you carry around every day. Is this how you want to spend your life?

The Ultimate Eating Program

In this chapter on weight control, I emphasize the importance of what we put in our mouths. Generally speaking, we cannot go wrong with fresh fruits and vegetables, especially when they are grown organically. But what is the IDEAL food choice, I am often asked.

One of my clients is the world-renowned Hippocrates Health Institute in West Palm Beach, Florida – rated the top medical wellness spa in the world. A vegan diet consisting primarily of organic raw and living foods is the foundation of their educational programs, which are inspiring, enriching and life-saving.

I have personally witnessed people with "terminal" and other illnesses make full recoveries and lead productive and healthy lives. Tumors disappear, glycemic levels and PSA counts normalize, and cholesterol levels drop 70 points, and sometimes within just weeks.

For more than 30 years, Dr. Brian Clement, Director of Hippocrates Health Institute, has taught that a meat-, dairy- and sugar free intake of 80 percent raw, living organic foods is optimal for health. He adds that cooking foods above 115 degrees destroys the precious enzymes that are so vital to the building and repair of cells and tissues. The Hippocrates Program also emphasizes the importance of rest, exercise, and stress reduction techniques for an optimal life style.

I have not eaten red meat, veal or poultry since 1973. Since attending their nine-week Health Educator Program, I have made additional changes to my eating regimen. Now I "think green" when I grocery shop, and start each morning with a combination drink of organic celery, cucumber and parsley. I am now drinking two ounces of wheatgrass juice in addition to my morning juice and avoid solid foods until after 11 a.m. I've also added raw living sprouts – that I grow myself – to my salads, as well as digestive enzyme supplements.

Now, I can personally vouch for the program. Once detoxifying from preservatives and additives (chemicals) found in most store bought prepared foods, practically everyone I knew in the program felt and looked 10 years younger. You can read more about this program and my experience on my website, www.stressreduction.com.

While the Hippocrates program is ideal, most people find it extremely challenging to eat and live this way, especially once they leave the supportive and controlled environment of the 45-acre tropical campus. We may not be able to "do it all," but we can make gradual changes to our diet, and move to a higher level of consciousness. They key is education and action.

Begin now to take small steps toward permanent lifestyle changes. You will not only feel better, but you will slow the aging process, and reverse and avoid many painful diseases.

The Raisin Trick

Here's one more thing to think about before you eat that raisin. What did it take for the raisin to reach your lips? A seed was planted in the ground; it was watered and drenched by the sun as it grew on a vine along with the other grapes. It was harvested, dried, packaged, shipped, and placed on the shelf where you reached for it and put it in your cart. You paid for it and brought it home to teach you a lesson about being mindful. It's a symphony of nature and humanity, and yet we take what we eat for granted, not stopping long enough to appreciate the raisin's journey. Think of it as an analogy for your own life

Take a moment now and put those raisins in your mouth one at a time. Think about your own life as the flavor of the raisin is released in your mouth. What are the dynamics that make you want to eat food that you know is not healthy, food that will eventually lead to diabetes, illness, and death? You don't see many fat old people. Is this what you really want?

As you swallow, give thanks for being alive and having the power to make changes in your life. This will release stress and unhappiness that keeps you bound to mindless eating. When you do that you will find yourself on the right path to health and wellness. You'll also find that happiness is right behind you waiting to come inside your house.

Rx #15: Do the Raisin Trick whenever you feel stressed, anxious or sad and you feel compelled to eat.

Chapter 3

OVERCOMING SEXUAL STRESS

"An intellectual is a person who has found one thing that's more interesting than sex." – Aldous Huxley

A Quiz: THE SEX O-METER

Prudes, prostitutes, strippers and saints all have one thing in common: They are sexual beings. But we all have different libidos and varying sexual needs, so it's easy to understand how difficult it can be to have a mutually satisfying sexual experience with one partner for the long haul. If one partner is highly sexual and the other isn't, then no matter how great the attraction, stress may arise.

The following quiz will help you decide if you are taking personal responsibility for your sexuality. If you must know the truth, it is really up to YOU to let go and enjoy the pleasure of intimacy or orgasm. (If you're not currently in an intimate relationship, think of your most recent partner, or just think of your relationships in general, when answering each question.)

In this quiz we are evaluating your level of sexual stress. There are no right or wrong answers. When answering the question, become aware of the amount of stress associated with the issue you are considering. Your answers may provide clues as to how much stress there is in your life around sex.

Can you have an orgasm with a partner?   Yes or No

Do you require a sex toy or something other than your partner to
have an orgasm?   Yes or No

Do you feel in sync with your partner?   Yes or No

Does your partner take sufficient time to bring you to orgasm?
                                                         Yes or No

Do you desire your partner?   Yes or No

Do you feel resentful of your partner when it comes to sex?
                                                         Yes or No

Do you fantasize about other people during the sex act?
                                                         Yes or No

Do you feel sex is an obligation in your relationship instead of
something you look forward to?   Yes or No

Would you rather not have sex with your current partner?
                                                         Yes or No

Good Sex Makes the World Go Round

Air, food and sex are three of our most basic human needs, but sex is by far the most complicated. While we can breathe alone and eat alone, coupling takes two people. Sex, like food, also has an emotional component. As such, the act of sex can take us to extreme joy and great heights and also plunge us into deep despair.

The upside is that sex is a good stress reliever. Sexual activity is not only pleasurable, but it stimulates the heart, the immune system and brain function, and promotes longevity. Since the mind and body are so closely connected, it stands to reason that our brains bring about sexual desire. Sex experts say that it all starts in the brain.

Some men feel they can take medication like Viagra, Levitra or Cialis to get an erection, and there are a lot of men who do exactly that for recreational sex. If there is no desire in the brain, however, then you will NOT get an erection. Sex is all about the brain and has to do with natural chemicals such as endorphins, oxytocin and dopamine.

The state of biochemical stimulation produced by the release of these endorphins at orgasm causes the production of white blood cells, which strengthens immunity. The profound sense of relaxation that people experience after sex becomes an antidote to the stress itself. After sex, the muscles relax and tension ebbs from the body, creating an overall sense of well-being. Some women feel such a boost of energy after sex that they can play a game of tennis or run five miles.

Positive moods promote good immune functioning and recovery from illness, while negative moods such as anger, depression and fear contribute to a myriad of physical and emotional problems. Studies have shown that couples who report sharing satisfactory sex lives have fewer arguments and conflicts due to the intimacy and connection they feel. Couples who are happy together in bed are likely to be happy together in life.

Conversely, while an orgasm can put us into a state of deep relaxation, stress in a relationship can invade and interfere with the pleasurable aspects of sex. This can send a couple into a tailspin, resulting in quiet depression, a deep depression or even a trip to the divorce lawyer.

Sexual stress is more common than you can imagine. Men worry about sexual performance and women are often concerned about being attractive or not having their emotional needs met. Almost everyone has some fear relating to sex and almost everyone will experience arousal problems at some point in time.

According to statistics, 25 percent of all Americans will experience little or no sexual desire at some time in their life. It is how you deal with this situation that can make the difference.

Knowing these statistics does little to help couples whose sexual dysfunction threatens to destroy their relationship. As a population, we've always had fears, guilt, and self-consciousness when it comes to sex. In the past few decades our society has become more candid and aware of sex, to the point of obsession. Look around you: It's all about sex.

Fifty years ago, Elvis was not allowed to do pelvic thrusts in public while singing his rock 'n' roll hits. Today, cable stations offer full frontal nudity and graphic X-rated movies. Sex is everywhere – in magazine ads, on larger than life billboards, in songs and in movies – especially in movies such as Lie with Me, The Brown Bunny, The Dreamers and Wild Orchid, and in television shows like Sex in the City and Lipstick Jungle.

But sex is life and life is sex. Without sex we would not exist, and yet there still exists a resistance to discussing sexual problems, even with therapists.

There are many situations that can cause sex-related stress. Fear of intimacy can be tied to something that a person witnessed in childhood and does not understand fully. Or they may resist intimacy at a primal level and need to discover the cause of this resistance.

Fran's Story – "Ho-Hum" Sex

Fran was in her twenties and living with a human sex machine – a man who wanted sex morning, noon and night. Although they had been together for three years, Fran had never experienced orgasm and was filled with resentment. Then she met Luke, 15 years her senior, and they began an affair.

"He had a very low libido, which was such a relief because I didn't want sex that often," Fran told me. "But when we had sex it was good. He knew just how to make me scream with delight and I no longer thought I was frigid or that there was something wrong with me."

It often happens that a sexual problem is partner specific. In that case, the problem disappears when the individuals find partners who are better suited for them.

In time, Luke's libido dropped even lower until they were having sex only three times a year. "It's a miracle that we managed to have two children, "Fran joked. "But after awhile it began eating away at me because he would enjoy his girlie magazines and get off that way, which made me feel really undesirable."

Although she kept herself in shape after the birth of her second child, sex disappeared altogether from their marriage. Fran, who felt a sense of frustration and loss of love, moved out of their bed and onto the living room couch.

"How could I sleep with a man who was so rejecting?" she asks. "He'd rather have an airbrushed photo of a cosmetically enhanced bimbo than the real thing!"

"You seem angry," I observed.

"I am angry – and disappointed – and my self-esteem is in the toilet. Why should I stay in a marriage that is so unfulfilling?"

"Does that mean it's over?" I asked. "Have you expressed this to him? Does he see this as a problem? If so is he willing to change?"

It is important in relationships to talk about what's bothering you, especially if you are thinking about leaving the relationship. When you express your feelings and talk about what you need, there is a good chance that you can stay together – provided that both of you are willing to compromise.

When two people are in a long-term committed relationship, married or not, things change and so do their needs. As the love between them grows (or diminishes), so does the sex. The ho-hum factor sets in and stress levels begin to rise. If one partner feels the need to stray outside the marriage, or asks their mate to do something that makes them uncomfortable, anxiety can be heightened even more.

Renee, an attractive 49-year old, came to see me when her relationship with her second husband, Jim, soured after two years of marriage.

"I'm not an exhibitionist," she told me. "I dress conservatively because I don't like people leering at my breasts or legs. But Jim gets turned on when other men see me in provocative clothing."

To keep Jim happy, Renee began wearing see-through blouses even though she felt cheap and compromised. Over time, and much to Renee's surprise, those feelings began to change.

"At first I started getting turned on knowing that Jim was aroused," she said. "Then that changed."

Renee began reading about exhibitionism and voyeurism and learned that with sex anything goes, but it still didn't sit well with her.

"I'm going along for the ride to keep our marriage intact," she said. "But everything in our life now revolves around sex – the movies we see, the books we read, and Internet porn sites. I'm stressed-out about it. So do I go along with it and let men ogle me in public in my skimpy outfits, or do I refuse to go along with it and watch my marriage fall apart?"

Renee's dilemma is not unusual. In this instance it was the indelible imprint of Renee's Catholic upbringing that made her feel guilty about the situation. Jim wasn't asking her to have sex with other men – he just wanted to show off his bride. But Renee didn't see it that way.

As our sessions progressed, I helped Renee see that having fantasies was perfectly normal. She realized that her ideas could be the direct result of her strict Catholic upbringing and that if she could see it differently, it might become acceptable to indulge her husband in his fantasy. It is important to note, however, that if the woman is uncomfortable with this arrangement, then a compromise needs to be worked out. There are safe ways to meet everyone's needs.

Renee decided to override her fear and take a chance. She went to the beach in a very revealing bathing suit. Her husband loved it and she loved the way he looked at her. Instead of feeling cheap or debased, she felt adored and admired, and her marriage became stronger and more loving without anyone getting hurt or feeling used.

Rx #16: Anything of a sexual nature that puts you outside your comfort level is a topic for discussion with your partner. You need not let anyone shame, humiliate, or push you into doing something you don't want to do just to save the relationship.

The sexual "code" in our country has become much more relaxed over the past few decades. Things once thought taboo (pregnant women posing nude on a magazine cover) are now acceptable. Baby boomers and generation X and Y don't want to be judged or stymied by their sexual behavior anymore. Young people today are much more candid about sex and seem to be less inhibited – perhaps more so than the flower children of the 60's.

Sandy's Story – Surprising Sex

Sandy was young and playful and madly in love with her partner, Tom. She understood his preoccupation with sexual acts, and rather than resist, she decided to accommodate him when he least expected it.

"We were driving on the Florida Turnpike to the Keys for the weekend and when we approached a toll booth I dove into the back seat and took of all my clothes. There I was, stark naked on my back, fully exposed to the young toll clerk," she told me.

Since Tom constantly pushed Sandy to be more erotic on the spur of the moment she gave him what he wanted.

"How did he react?" I asked. "Did he pull over and jump on you?"

Sandy's face fell. "Actually, he was embarrassed and didn't think what I did was amusing. What's that all about?"

"What we think we want and what we get can be very confusing, "I explained. "Think about the man who wants a threesome and then he's disappointed when it happens. Sometimes the fantasy is better than the reality."

Rx #17: Taking risks and being spontaneous in sex can stimulate sexual growth and open new vistas, or it can backfire. Explore what works best for you and your partner.

It's important to view sex without fear and self-consciousness. After all, who's doing the judging? We need to have new conversations about sex – truthful and honest discussions about what pleases us and what doesn't. Above all, an honest talk about your needs, desires, and sexual boundaries must be conveyed to your partner.

As you probably know firsthand, men and women often differ in their approach to sex. Men can go immediately from cold to hot while some women are like an oven – they require pre-heating. Some men prefer to just have sex while many women like to make love, have foreplay, experience romance and the tenderness that goes along with it. But it is true that both can be enjoyable for both sexes.

For some older women, there may be a need for lubrication. Also, extended intercourse might be painful unless the body is primed. Experts suggest that engaging in at least a half hour of kissing, stroking and cuddling pumps up the exhilaration factor for both men and women, making the sex more enjoyable.

Rx #18: Slow down. Don't rush through the sexual act. Foreplay, stroking, cuddling and kissing will lead to more satisfactory lovemaking for both parties.

Many guys trade in a car after two years, even though the car is running fine. They buy bigger TV's with plasma screens and high definition. They buy electronic gadgets that can communicate in every conceivable way. And yet they cannot communicate with their partner. If they're looking for something (or someone) different they may go to strip clubs, hang out in the porn section of movie rental stores, or buy X-rated magazines. But men are not the only ones looking for a change of pace.

Interestingly, the number of women who are pursuing affairs is increasing. Infidelity has been known to raise the stress level for everyone concerned, because it brings a whole new set of problems. The key to avoiding this stress is to keep the spice inside the relationship instead of pursuing excitement outside the relationship.

The "Ho-Hum" Effect

Jack and Jane came to see me when they began having trouble in their marriage. It was Jack's second marriage and Jane's third, and they wanted to keep the relationship intact. Jack wanted to please Jane in bed, but the length of time it took Jane to reach orgasm was difficult for Jack. It often left him feeling overwhelmed and frustrated. Jane was frustrated that Jack was impatient and wouldn't take the time to satisfy her.

"I feel that since she can't reach orgasm, she doesn't love me," he told me. As a result of his frustration Jack pulled back physically from Jane, leaving her feeling he didn't love her. Although Jane wanted to be more romantic, she became angry that Jack stopped initiating sex. She told him that she didn't care if they ever had sex again because he didn't do it right. Even more frustrated and angry, Jack went on the internet looking for sex and found it. Jane asked for a divorce.

"This is typical sex stress," I told them. "When sex gets separated from love, it creates anxiety and negative feelings".

All too often a marriage or long-term relationship falls into a groove as partners get lazy and start taking each other for granted. Jack was typical of that syndrome. He didn't want to spend the time to please Jane, rationalizing that she was unable to be satisfied.

"It's important to know what turns on your lover or partner," I told both of them. "Guessing leads to false assumptions and communication is the only way to prevent feelings of anger, guilt, frustration, and ultimately stress."

Jane's reaction was not uncommon in this situation. She belittled Jack by saying he "didn't do it right" and he reacted by saying that she didn't want sex. The withholding of affection is a detrimental response to any couple, which creates even more stress.

"I have a job," Jack explained during one of our sessions. "I'm a mechanic. I tune up cars all day and I don't want another job tuning up Jane before we have sex."

"So you want to turn a key and have me climax?" she replied angrily. "It doesn't work that way."

"When I'm tired I just want to have sex, "Jack retorted. "Uncomplicated, simple, caveman sex. I don't want to know what's wrong; I just want to get laid."

Rx #19: It takes a lot of patience to be a successful lover, and it's an active process that can take years to perfect. Most successful lovers enjoy pleasing their partners and want to know how to do so.

Making love in the same way, in the same place, on the same nights or in the same position, often stifles the romance. Couples forget that they often need romance before the sexual act. They may even feel that tenderness is something they no longer need now that the honeymoon is over.

The biggest complaint I hear from women is: "He expects me to just do it – even when he smells bad and hasn't shaved or brushed his teeth. That's just disrespectful. And once he is satisfied, he immediately falls asleep, leaving me unfulfilled."

Since there are so many variables that come into play when two people are intimate, there's no way to cover them all in one chapter. So here are a few things to pay attention to when approaching this critical sexual dysfunction junction.

What Men Need to Know About Women

Women need kissing and cuddling. You cannot always pop a Viagra and get right to it. Think of foreplay as the appetizer before the main course.

It's important to remember that women's needs are different from men's. They need to feel sexy and aroused, which usually happens during foreplay. Although there are plenty of lubricants on the market, only a natural secretion from the woman's body will sustain the sex act over a period of time.

Women (and often older men) have a greater need for emotional stroking in addition to physical stroking. Sexual self-esteem becomes more of an issue when a woman or man reaches their fifties and can often escalate as one ages.

A man can make a woman feel sexy by telling her how much she turns him on and holding steady eye contact. He can also make her feel loved by appreciating her, and not just as a sexual partner.

Women need more emotional intimacy than men. There is a spiritual exchange that needs to take place before a meaningful sexual connection occurs. For some men, but for most women, they need to feel they're reaching a higher plane than a quickie roll in the sack provides. They connect with the heart and head before sex even factors into the equation.

Rx #20: To build intimacy, start by opening the lines of communication. Share a desire and encourage your partner to do the same. Studies have shown that telling your partner what you want in bed leads to deeper emotional intimacy. Enjoy time together without interruption, both in and out of the bedroom, to promote a connection.

What Women Need to Know About Men

While women need physical stroking to get warmed up, men often require verbal stroking before, during and even after sex. As a man gets older he may require more physical stimulation due to physical changes. Sexual health and mental well-being is also dependent on physical factors such as high blood pressure or diabetes, and may play a role in what is required to stimulate the man.

Young men (womanizers in particular) often don't care how they perform as long as they add a notch to their belts. But as men mature, fulfilling a woman's sexual needs becomes more important and being a considerate lover adds to their sense of pride. Since sex requires two people, it stands to reason that the more positive reinforcement a man receives from his partner, the more loving he will become. Positive (and passionate) reinforcement sends the message to a man that he is fulfilling her needs – and that's a good thing for the man.

If your partner is not touching you the right way, tell him what you need, NOT what turns you off. Some men like hearing a woman moan, sigh and groan. It tells him he's on the right track. If a woman is not making sounds, the man might think his partner is not enjoying herself. But some women are just quiet during the sexual act, and it does not mean that they are unhappy with their partner's performance. Discussing this often helps to ease concerns a partner may have.

Communicate...Communicate...Communicate

It is vital that couples communicate what they want and keep a positive and gentle dialogue.

When a man has trouble performing, some women blame themselves. She might verbalize it by saying, "Don't you find me sexy?" or "Don't I turn you on anymore?" Those insecurities can add to a man's performance problems, but in reality erectile dysfunction (ED) is a fact of life which can occur in men of any age and for any reason. Alcohol, drugs, tobacco, obesity, and overwork all play a part in the dynamics of ED.

In addition, men tend to pressure themselves to perform at peak levels every time. With the bar set so high, it's natural that things sometimes go awry. It has been found that when a man has trouble performing, it can add an extra burden to his future love-making experience.

It is important for men to know this and take the pressure off their partners. He's already beating himself up over it. If you're making demands or complaining that you're not satisfied, his sense of failure will be overwhelming and the downward spiral might continue. Even with ED medication, which can address the physical functioning during the sex act, underlying issues need to be discussed to encourage and maintain a healthy sex life.

RX #21: A man wants a partner who accepts him even when he cannot perform. So if things don't go as planned, don't make a big deal about it or get stressed. Make him feel emotionally safe, even when he has trouble performing. This is true for both partners, inside and outside the bedroom. Feeling accepted for one's faults and failures is what builds intimacy and keeps it in place.

To help move through the ED experience, explore new avenues of pleasure or watch an erotic move. Surprise you partner with something spontaneous: A striptease, a sex toy, a video or book, a new position – anything out of the ordinary. The only thing holding you back from getting out of a sexual rut is your imagination.

Sex toys can be a part of a couple's repertoire. Why not go together to an adult toy store and look at the possibilities? That can be fun for both partners and can also help them discuss what they prefer when it comes to toys, lotions, oils and more.

Do you remember the scene in the movie Fried Green Tomatoes in which Kathy Bates wraps herself in Saran Wrap to spice up her marriage? It was a funny moment, and it was the right idea. By changing your appearance with a wig, your partner will feel he's with another woman – that's OK, because he's with YOU. He may even love you more if you're willing to add fun and excitement to your sexual life.

Men usually don't need encouragement to go to an adult toy store, and if he takes you there it might be a clue that he thinks you're sexy. It also means he is encouraging you to be his seductress and lover. Instead of being insulted that you are not sexy enough, consider it as a compliment because what he's really saying is: "I want you more than anyone else because you turn me on. I love you, not some stranger twirling around a pole or on the cover of a magazine".

Rx #22: Boring sex is a death sentence when it comes to passion. Keep the spark alive with spontaneity, new ideas, positions, locations, or the use of magazines or X-rated movies. Anything that takes both of you away from the sexual routine and into something new and exciting will invigorate your sexual experience

My first book, *Go Naked to the Market* (www.stressreduction.com), didn't literally mean take off your clothes and walk into the supermarket. But you should be willing to strip off all the falseness and walk down the street emotionally naked if that's what it takes to get to the truth.

Cornelia's Story – High Anxiety

For Cornelia, getting naked was a big deal. Cornelia was an attractive and successful woman who traveled around the world on business. But she had insecurities about her body – and a negative self-image – stemming from small asymmetrical breasts and a childhood appendix scar. We talked about it during our sessions and she decided to do something drastic about it.

"I equated nudity with sex...the naked state with sex," she told me. "If you are naked it has to be in a sexual context. But I found this idea was holding me back from fully experiencing life."

Cornelia booked a trip to Mexico, and part of the program included being naked in a ceremonial swear lodge. Although she was tired of her fears, Cornelia couldn't get past her negativity about nudity, and didn't finish the sweat lodge ceremony.

When she came to see me after the trip she was in a high state of frustration and stress. We talked about her feelings for a few weeks, and one day she came into my office with a huge grin.

"I found a nudist resort," she said, waving a pamphlet. "And my friend Bill said he'd come with me. It's over Halloween weekend so we'll be in costume. I think it's the perfect way to deal with this."

When she returned I asked how it went.

"It worked for me," she said. "I didn't have to be totally naked, we had costumes and we could get as undressed as we wanted. Some people were totally naked, but there was no pressure."

I asked how she felt.

"It didn't evoke the anxiety I thought it would, "she said. "Growing up, I was taught that being naked was shameful, but now I see that nudity and sex don't have to go hand-in-hand. Being naked just for the sake of being naked was a liberating experience.

Rx #23: Nobody is perfect – not even the airbrushed models in the men's magazines. So lighten up!

Scars show character. Love-handles happen to everyone sooner or later. Breasts are breasts – some big, some small, some sag. Nipples come in every size, shape, and color. The same goes for penises. It's not all about the size. Even if you have a few wrinkles or sags, you're still perfect in your own special way. The people who matter understand this.

Achieving Mindful Sex

Like Cornelia and Renee, millions of men and women were taught that nudity and sex are bad. Some religions still preach outdated, negative views of nudity and sex. This can be very stressful. Something as beautiful and healthy as sex deserves better. It's a strange paradox, and sad for those who feel constrained by these limitations.

Renee was the product of a strict upbringing, which is the reason she didn't want to wear a see-through blouse for her husband – even though many would view it as harmless flirtation.

"My father was very strict about the clothes I wore and would tell me that men were lustful evil creatures who would try to steal my virginity. He said I should keep my legs crossed and think holy thoughts. I still hear his voice in my head although I know there's nothing wrong with showing some cleavage or wearing a short skirt and high heels. That doesn't make me a slut."

Unfortunately, most problems aren't as easy to resolve as Renee's and Cornelia's.

Fran felt she could not live without sex and her husband refused to provide it. "The night he told me to care for my sexuality myself was the beginning of the end," she told me. "What choice did I have? Basically he was telling me that he wouldn't have sex with me.

He could have masturbated with me – at least it would have been a gesture, and it would have kept us in the same bed. But he didn't."

After leaving her husband, Fran embarked on a series of brief affairs to help boost her self-esteem and sexual prowess.

"It wasn't very satisfactory, but it was better than feeling rejected," she told me. "Eventually I met someone who was on the same sexual wavelength. We had sex three times a week instead or three times a day or three times a year. And it was great sex."

So what can you do to enjoy sex when you're stressed out or not in the mood? Here are a few suggestions to override any libido inhibitor.

➢ *Eat healthy and avoid overeating.* Studies show that a balanced diet of protein, carbohydrates, fresh fruits and vegetables can decrease stress. Have several small meals throughout the day.

➢ *Change your routines.* If you always have sex at the same time, at the same place and same way, try something new. Get out of the box.

➢ *Get away.* Even if you spend only one night in a hotel away from the phone, computer and kids, it's a great way to reestablish the connection the two of you once had. If you can manage more than one night, that's even better.

➢ *Exercise.* Even 15 minutes of brisk walking releases feel-good hormones and gives you extra energy.

➢ *Flirt.* Flirting puts people in a good mood and acts as a sexual warm-up. Flirting includes paying compliments, making teasing comments or light-hearted jokes, and talking about fantasies you would like to do together. It even works for couples who have been together a long time, and it adds a playful quality.

➤ *Take a bath together.* Not only does the warmth increase blood flow to the genitals, but the foreplay can make the sex act even more enjoyable. For something new and different, try having sex in the tub.

➤ *Organize your life.* When you are stressed with commitments and overloaded with obligations, it's extremely difficult to relax and get in the mood.

➤ *Think sex thoughts.* Your brain is just as important as your genitals when it comes to sex. Rent an X-rated movie or read erotic literature. It's amazing how turned on you can get with a silly but sexy novel.

➤ *Be considerate of your partner.* Do something sweet and unexpected. Serve a candlelit dinner, bring home flowers, have a bottle of champagne waiting.

➤ *Give compliments.* When you notice something you like, make a positive comment. Does he or she have nice hair or great eyes? A fine figure or beautiful hands? Compliments are often the key to success in romantic endeavors.

➤ *Clean yourself up.* It may sound trite, but smelling good is a major turn-on for both men and women. Personal hygiene is an important factor that's too often overlooked.

➤ *Touch and stroke one another for no reason at all.*

➤ *Laugh hard and often.* Laughing is more than a stress reliever; it helps you relax and unwind and provides a common bond with your partner.

➤ *Set the mood.* If you want a romantic encounter, encourage it with dim lighting, scented candles and mellow music. Sexy lingerie can't hurt either.

➤ *Take it slow.* Loosen each other up with mutual massages or foot rubs. Stroke each other lightly in a non-sexual way, moving your hands closer to the erotic areas of the body. Add kissing and licking. Share fantasies. Great sex is all about communication.

➤ *If you have a headache, take an aspirin.* Don't use it as an excuse to skip sex!

RX #24: The best sex is the result of open communication. If you are experiencing a problem with your partner, talk about it – but not in the bedroom. Don't hide under the covers and pretend it's not there, because problems don't simply disappear. If you cannot resolve the situation, seek professional help with a therapist or sex counselor.

Learning to Manage Sexual Stress

More than anything else, human beings want to be loved. Ironically, the intimacy of love is also what we fear the most. There are even words that describe this fear – Philophobia (fear of being in love), aphenphosmphobia (fear of being touched), and erotophobia (fear of sex).

For various reason some people are unable or unwilling to share personal thoughts and feelings with others. When two people disagree, resolution is not always easy or obvious. You have several options:

1. Put up a wall. Become obstinate, turn your back, leave the house, go to sleep, or escape through the internet.

2. Wait for you partner to acquiesce and do it your way – or apologize.

3. Explore your inner self and accept your shortcomings – and then begin to forgive yourself for being human. Obviously, this is the wisest choice.

Withdrawing from romantic relationships, refusing to touch, be touched or kissed can be a symptom of childhood rejection. Low self-esteem can make a person feel defective or unworthy of receiving love. Conflict can then become the method of loving in a relationship.

Jane and Jack are the perfect example of loving through conflict. Jack was angry, not only at Jane, but in general. He was stressed out at his job and brought those hostile feelings home to his wife. When Jane didn't have an orgasm in a specific period of time, Jack got angry. Jack's reaction was clearly inappropriate and could easily drive a wedge between them. In this case, it would be best if Jack handled his anxiety about work before jumping into bed.

Recognizing that we all have differences – and limitations – can be useful for understanding and accommodating our differences. With some encouragement from Jane, and a frank discussion about what she found most pleasurable, Jack and Jane could have worked out their problems before coming to see me.

"There's nothing wrong with using a vibrator to get you to the point of climax," I told Jane. "It's all right even if you have to do it yourself while Jack watches. In fact, he may find it exciting to watch you please yourself."

Jack's face lit up when I suggested this, and even though Jane wasn't thrilled with the idea she agreed to try it.

"You can't expect Jack to take all the responsibility for this," I said. "Sex is a highway and to have great sex you both need to be going in the same direction."

Jane decided to venture outside her comfort zone and experiment with the vibrator. She discovered a new pleasure in sex.

By sharing their likes and dislikes, Jane and Jack discovered better forms of communication that brought them more peace and pleasure at home.

Rx #25: Sexual stress is usually a symptom of other conflicts within the partnership. Instead of being afraid to deal with your anger, learn to keep it out of your relationship. For example, if your boss is giving you grief, don't let it seep into your bedroom. Find ways to diffuse the issues with your boss so that you can enjoy your partner.

The kiss of death in a relationship is when you bring old emotional baggage into the mix. Some people treat their sexual partners with such disdain and resentment that it's a wonder there is any enjoyment at all! Romantic intimacy is about pleasure, fun, relaxation, healing, and connecting with another human being. Do not talk about your bad relationships, gas prices, bar fights or work frustrations. Focus on the good times you have with your partner instead of the bad times you had during the day. Don't bring negativity home with you.

Rx #26: Moments that seem important at the time are often just a blip on the screen of eternal life. So let negativity go and forgive conflicts without judgment, allowing the conflict to dissipate into nothingness.

To reduce sexual stress in a relationship there must be variety, spontaneity, vitality, exploration, and an omnipresent sense of excitement to nurture and nourish the body and mind. The underlying foundation is communication.

A 38-year-old woman came to see me to address her chronic fatigue syndrome. Angie felt tired and achy all the time. She also felt twice her age.

"I don't have any energy," she told me. "I can't focus on conversations even with my best friends. I don't want to socialize and I'm always depressed. I used to be the life of the party. Now I feel like I've been run over by a truck."

I've learned from experience that when my clients make an appointment the reason they give is often a far cry from what's troubling them. Appointments like Angie's are a cry for help. A deep-seated negative emotion is almost always the root cause of disease. We call this stress.

"Why are you really here?" I asked.

Angie stared at me until tears filled her eyes. "My husband and I don't have sex anymore," she said. "I'm afraid he's going to find a younger woman. We've been together since high school and nothing happens anymore. I'm so frustrated and anxious."

As our discussion progressed, she recalled that her frustration and fatigue started around the time that her husband started bringing home erotic videos for them to watch together.

Angie didn't think he was cheating, yet she was disturbed at his decline in affection. There were not intimate gestures or playful touching, and intercourse had become a thing of the past.

Greg's love for Angie held steady throughout their 20-year marriage. His earlier fears and bouts of jealousy had been replaced with maturity, ease and calm. But, he found himself yearning for the passion that they had at the beginning of their relationship. Angie badly wanted to rekindle the flame.

Greg thought Angie was an incredibly sexy woman and they had an emotional bond that would be impossible to find with a one-night affair. The women in the erotic films he saw represented a fantasy that included Angie.

Greg was frustrated in his attempt to get Angie to dress provocatively, visit a nude beach or experiment with sex toys. The more Angie balked, the more sexually stressed Greg became. Her doubts and low self-esteem escalated with her passivity and body pain.

"I feel cheapened and self-conscious," she told me. "The harder he tries to get me to loosen up, the more I dig my heels in."

Unfortunately, Angie and Greg's story is all too common. And yet it is important to have safe outlets so sex does not become a stressful component of the relationship.

With the advent of worldwide communication systems that include internet sex sites, societal taboos are becoming obsolete. Though sexual behavior is more open and permissive, change doesn't come swiftly and resistance can still cause conflict or stress.

Once Greg and Angie came together and openly communicated their feelings to one another, they started a new dialogue. It was after that they both agreed to be more open and adventuresome in restoring their sexuality.

Rx #27: Ask for what you want. Asking does not guarantee you will get it, but it certainly improves your chances. Show or tell your lover what things excite you the most. If your partner needs convincing, take baby steps toward your ultimate goal.

While there is no way I can cover every problem of a sexual nature in this section, here are some helpful examples of ways to control the level of stress and anxiety you and your partner may experience:

➢ The difference between immature romantic intimacy and adult romantic intimacy is that adults learn to control their impulses. Unfortunately, too many adults act sex-crazed and immature long after it is acceptable. Sexual excitement is no excuse for trying to force someone to do things that make him or her uncomfortable. When your partner says "no" to something, accept their feelings gracefully and do not berate them or act abusively. Instead, get to know your partner by asking them what they like or dislike.

➢ Communicate clearly about what you like and dislike. The things you find to be a turn-on may be a complete turn-off to your partner. Remember the story of Sandy and Tom? She did what she thought he'd like (lying naked in the back seat of the car) but Tom was not turned on by her behavior. That left Sandy confused and angry. Sex can be a challenging issue to resolve because it is laden with emotional problems from the past. Become OK with the process of discovery and enjoy learning about your partner.

➢ No matter what, don't blame yourself when there is a miscommunication, a difference in your libidos or an intimacy problem. It takes two to tango.

➢ Some of the sexiest words in any language are "please," "thank you," and "you're welcome." No matter what the situation, politeness shows that you respect your partner and value his or her company. Your positive energy will make your partner trust you and become more open to new and exciting things in your relationship.

➢ If you'd rather not have sex with your partner, then consider ending the intimate component of the relationship. Remember, sex and love usually go together, yet they can be mutually exclusive. Regardless, the key to stress-free sex is letting go, taking personal responsibility, and enjoying oneself without being attached to the outcome.

Rx #28: There is no past or future. There is only the now! Live in the moment.

The Lotus Bliss Exercise

Changing your partner's behavior or attitude toward sex can be a daunting task. Sometimes, such as in Fran's case, there is nothing you can do. Although she and her husband went for counseling, she realized that her husband would never change. Sex was not on his list of priorities, so the only way for her to find satisfaction was to get out of the marriage. Some couples, like Jack and Jane, work through their issues and manage their bedroom stress.

Whether or not you choose to stay and deal with the situation or get out of it, there are ways to reduce the stress you feel about it. Here is a simple meditation that may help. I call it The Lotus Bliss.

The most essential exercises for men and women are Kegal exercises, which are guaranteed to improve the quality of your sex and promote orgasm. This daily meditative exercise strengthens the pubococcygeus (PC) muscle and is especially recommended as a prelude to foreplay. I call this exercise a "meditation in motion" because it is necessary to pay full attention and focus on the exercise. In addition, many other health related problems such as incontinence can be helped and or prevented through the strengthening in the PC muscles.

Considered the ultimate meditation in motion for good sex, Kegels are prescribed by doctors for vaginal tightness after childbirth. Learning how to contract and release the PC muscles can provide benefits in sexual performance in both men and women and increase sexual enjoyment.

Here's how you do Kegels: The PC muscle is located in the genital area. It is the muscle used when stopping the flow of urine. Contract the PC muscle 20 times- one squeeze per second. Slowly exhale while tightening the muscles around your genitals – including the anus. Do not contract the buttocks, and do not bear down during the release, just let go. Start with two sets of 20 contractions a day, gradually increasing to two sets of 75 a day.

A Bed Full of Love

There are a few additional pieces of advice worthy of mentioning to bring back that old loving feeling. Remember what happened in Rupert Holmes "The Pina Colada Song?" He and his lady had fallen into a rut, so he put a personal ad in the paper. He writes: "I like Pina Coladas and getting caught in the rain. I'm not much into health food, I am into champagne."

When he goes to meet the woman who responds, it's his lady. She says: "Oh, it's you." They laugh, and he says: "I never knew."

Once again, I hearken back to the word communication. It's the only way to work things out. Whether you choose to communicate with the help of a therapist or simply with each other, find a time and a space where you can be alone, with no computer, television, kids, or intrusions. Try taking a walk together and getting away from familiar surroundings to minimize distractions.

Remember too, that sex does not always have to be the result of a romantic evening. A physical connection does not necessarily mean two naked people in bed. A strong sexual relationship stems from a bond – a connection that happens with the head and the heart. And finally, try to find the playfulness and loving feeling that brought you together in the first place. Stay positively focused on the outcome. Remember that people can change and mistakes do happen. Know when to cut your losses and when to give love a second chance – and above all, trust your gut. That is the little voice inside you that knows what is best for you.

Spirituality and Sexuality

Throughout this chapter I have addressed issues overcoming sex stress created by a society where antiquated taboos predominate, guilt prevails over natural biological urges and suppressed desires cause relationship dysfunction. Sex is neither evil, dirty, not "the end all to be all." In fact, the highest measurement for great sex is spiritual.

First, let's take a look at the definition of "spiritual" which comes from the Latin "spirare," meaning to breathe. Just as our breath is our life force, so sex represents a natural agenda for life itself. We are sexual creatures and repression of natural biological releases can prove detrimental to our mental, emotional, physical and spiritual wellness.

Some people and institutions contend our current society is sexually obsessed and morally depraved. They believe that a decline in spiritual standards is due to internet porn, provocative clothing and emphasis on sexual content in movies and on television.

Yet change is inevitable. The pendulum invariably swings to explore, adjust and balance, just as witnessed during the ultra-conservative Victorian era. As free-willed individuals, we also go through phases as we age and mature. Sex is an integral aspect of this process.

History has proven so. Historically, Polynesians were sexually liberated. Remember the classic movie, "Mutiny on the Bounty?" The Englishmen went ashore on the exquisite island of Tahiti where sex was celebrated as an everyday wholesome part of life. Back home in England the climate was one where sex was encumbered by social forces and fornication considered grounds for burning in hell. The healthy island sexual code of conduct presented a freedom and joy not experienced by the crew. As a result, many chose to remain behind when the ship set sail compelled by an open and liberated lifestyle.

As a therapist, I work with individuals and couples on divisive sexual issues. I have learned there is more to sex than sex itself. Sex for sex sake usually won't sustain over time. Intimacy and communication, however, with a significant partner agreeing on sexual conduct will last indefinitely. The willingness to work, love, invent, create and enjoy sex as a team is truly fulfilling and spiritually evolutionary.

Fix your spiritual, emotional, mental and physical self and appropriate sexuality will usually follow. Hallelujah!

Chapter 4

FACING STRESS AT WORK

"He is richest who is content with the least, for content is the wealth of nature." – Socrates

A Quiz: HOW STRESSFUL IS YOUR WORK?

It's important to assess the source of your stress before you address it. Stress on the job is another thing that will take its toll on you, both at the workplace and at home. How stressed are you in your job? Answer these statements as either true or false, and then check the Stress Meter at the end to see how supported you are on the job.

1. My employer recognizes my talent and compliments me often.

True or False

2. My employer gives me steady pay raises and promotions.

True or False

3. I have many opportunities for career development at my current position.

True or False

4. I work for a company that values the individual worker.

True or False

5. My company provides stress-reducers. Like lunchtime workouts and massages.   True or False

If you answered True to more than three of the first five questions, you are one of the lucky Americans working today. You are the exception to the rule and I congratulate you on finding a job with relatively low stress levels.

Now consider these next five statements and again answer True or False.

6. I have tight deadlines and am constantly worried I'll miss one.

True or False

7. I work on a quota system and always feel I'm going to fall short.

True or False

8. There is no job security and I can be fired at any time (or I am self-employed).

True or False

9. My job is dangerous and I worry that I'll be hurt.

True or False

10. My job is so boring I could scream.

True or False

If you answered True to any of the last five questions, you should start thinking about finding another job or begin using the stress-reducing techniques in this chapter.

The Strain of Making Ends Meet

It doesn't matter if you are a CEO, a part-time employee, or in business for yourself, the pressure of a job can be enormous. Because most of us have to work for a living, this creates a constant and seemingly unavoidable problem. When the demands of a job cannot be met, the stage is set for illness, injury and failure. Even when a person enjoys the work, a job can turn negative and cause anxiety when things go wrong. At that point, any sense of satisfaction that you had can morph into feelings of stress and anxiety.

Unpleasant or dangerous conditions such as crowding, noise, air pollution, or difficulty with coworkers or superiors can have a harmful physical effect. As discussed in the first chapter, stress sets off an alarm in the brain, which responds by preparing the body for a defensive action. The nervous system is aroused and hormones are released to sharpen the senses, quicken the pulse, deepen respiration and tighten muscles. Because the flight-or-fight response is biologically programmed, everyone reacts in much the same way regardless of the underlying cause.

Short-lived or infrequent episodes of stress pose little risk. But when stressful situations continue day after day, year after year, the body is kept in a constant state of high alert. This intensifies the stress on our organs. Ultimately, fatigue or damage results and the ability of the body to repair and defend itself can become seriously compromised. That, in turn, raises the risk of injury or disease.

Some employees assume that stressful working conditions are a necessary evil. Some companies put a lot of pressure on their workers and ignore their health issues because they believe it is more profitable. But studies show that stressful working conditions are associated with increased absenteeism, tardiness and a high turnover rate.

In the past 20 years experts have analyzed the relationship between job stress and a variety of ailments such as mood and sleep disturbance, upset stomach and headache, and poor relationships with family and friends. The early signs of job stress and chronic disease are difficult to see because chronic diseases take a long time to develop. They can also be influenced by factors other than stress.

Nevertheless, evidence is mounting that suggests stress plays an important role in chronic health problems such as cardiovascular disease, musculoskeletal disorders and psychological troubles, as well as burn-out and depression. Stressful working conditions can also lead to more workplace injuries.

There are studies that suggest that stressful working conditions can cause suicide, cancer, ulcers and impaired immune function. The rage that a stressful job can elicit was named after a terrible shooting incident at a US Post Office by a disgruntled employee: It is now referred to as "going postal."

Some people cope with job stress better than others. What might be anxiety-provoking for one person may roll off the back of someone else. Although the importance of individual differences cannot be ignored, certain repetitive working conditions – such as assembly line work – are stressful to most people. Excessive workload demands and conflicting expectations are another key source of job stress. And that doesn't take into consideration stress factors at home and in our social life, or the dozens of small things that can go wrong in any day.

Audrey and Tom are social butterflies who have a wide circle of friends in Georgia and are always upbeat. Audrey works in a courtroom assisting prospective jurors, while Tom loads cargo onto planes at the airport – or did until a horrific motorcycle accident ended his career. As a result of the accident, Tom's seizures render him unable to work. The total financial burden came to rest on Audrey's shoulders.

"I've taken on extra work," she told me. "But it means I have to get up at 3:30 a.m. to get to work at 5." Audrey puts in four hours overtime before going to her regular job where she works until 6p.m. She also has a part-time weekend job.

"By the time I get home I'm almost too tired to eat," she adds. "I go to bed while it's still light outside. I don't know how I can keep this up, but what choice do I have if I have to pay all the bills?"

Audrey's story is typical of many families – they're overextended. If one spouse is ill, incapacitated, or for any reason cannot share the load, the responsibilities fall to the partner. Single parents can be stuck in the same rut too.

That is why it's important to strike a balance between work and family, personal life and social activities, while maintaining a relaxed and positive outlook. A network of friends and coworkers can help provide a support system.

Marion's Story – Working Misery

Marion is a 44-year-old single mom who left a stressful job as a legal secretary to become a full-time writer for a national magazine. She found the work very rewarding and enjoyed it immensely, despite a supervisor who was constantly breathing down her back and critiquing her work.

There were frequent editorial turnovers, and after a year Marion and many of her coworkers were fired in a company purge. "I know it's not because of my writing," she told me. But she was still very upset because she was the sole support of her family and child.

Marion applied for unemployment compensation and scraped by doing odd writing and editing jobs. She had to be very frugal and hated every minute of it. Her stress and anxiety level carried over in her sleep.

"I dream that I'm drowning," she told me. "The truth is that I'm drowning in debt."

Before her unemployment ran out, an editor at the magazine she had worked for asked her to work one day a week. Eventually that led to a full-time job.

"I have all the stress that I had with my previous work, but none of the perks like health insurance or vacation time," she complained. "And now I hear we're getting a new editor and everyone says he's awful."

I reminded Marion to stay in the NOW and not get ahead of herself. But the next time she saw me, she told me that the new editor was just as bad as she had heard.

"Brian is a micromanaging control freak who likes to humiliate and belittle us," she complained. "He doesn't like me at all and he hovers over my desk and demands information that I don't have. Or he will call me into his office and yell at me so the whole office can hear."

Marion was on the verge of a nervous breakdown. "I go to the office and I know I'm either going to faint or throw up. Every day is a misery. I live in such dread of being humiliated that I can't eat or enjoy time with my daughter. The weekends come and go in a fog, and by Sunday night I'm a total wreck because I'm dreading what's going to happen on Monday." Marion's situation is not unusual; many people dread Mondays for the same reason. Statistics show that it is the day of the week with the highest number of heart attacks.

Marion wrung her hands as we spoke. The tension was evident on her face and her shoulders were hunched. She looked as though she wanted to roll up into a ball.

"What do you do for relaxation?" I asked.

"I try to see a movie, but my head never stops spinning enough to enjoy it. I'm always trying to figure out how I'll survive if I'm fired again, because I no longer qualify for unemployment benefits."

I told Marion: Live each day and each moment as it comes. By focusing on what might happen, you lose connection with your body and the joy that is available now. Remember, most of what we fear about the future never occurs. Instead of dwelling on what is lacking, focus on what you have. Be grateful that you are able to work, that you have a job, and for other things like your daughter and your good health. Take the time to feel the gratitude deeply in your body. Then go for a walk or a swim with your daughter. These and similar activities help restore the mind/body balance.

Rx #29: Take responsibility for your situation. Get into a quiet place to find a solution for promoting your own personal wellness.

Customer-service work, which means listening to complaints from angry customers, is a highly stressful job. Laurie, a customer service clerk, is a 39-year-old married mother of two. She likes her job at the department store, and enjoys helping people and greeting them with a cheerful attitude.

During one of our group sessions, Laurie appeared distraught. She told us about a woman who came to the store and went into a tirade about a candle she bought. Since Laurie was not in a position to yell back at the customer and didn't want to provoke her any further, she internalized the abuse and was miserable the rest of the day. At home she took out her frustration on her husband and children. Later that night she realized she lost her positive attitude and had taken on the negative vibes of her customer. The candle was simply a catalyst that pushed her over the edge.

The lessons she learned in the stress clinic clarified her reactions and helped her to assess what she did and didn't want in a job. The following day, Laurie began searching the want ads for a new job, one that did not involve the stress associated with customer service.

This story illustrates how little it takes to make us unhappy. Work stress can impact your emotional and physical body, and negativity affect your ability to recognize it. Being unaware of stress prevents us from addressing the problem. That's why it is so important to be proactive and take responsibility for the situation. (Eventually Laurie found other work that was a better fit for her.)

I also learned about self-healing techniques in the company of masters of meditation and contemplation Ram Dass, Swamis Muktananda and Satchidananda and Thich Nhat Hanh. In their own ways they shared a constant theme: let go and "be here now."

I'm an old man who has known a great many problems, most of which never happened. – Mark Twain

I met Thich Nhat Hanh (the acclaimed teacher, poet, bestselling author, Buddhist monk and peace activist nominated by Martin Luther King for the Nobel Prize) in Key West, Florida, when he conducted a five-day retreat.

The retreat began in the pre-dawn hours. On the first day, Thich Nhat Hanh announced that the next three days would be observed in silence, except for the teachings (dharma talks) from him. All meals would be taken in silence beneath a gigantic tent at the edge of the site's golf course.

Each day, we gathered in the parking lot at 7 a.m. and he would begin a meditation walk across the golf course at a snail's pace, mindful of taking just one foot and one breath at a time.

And each day Thich Nhat Hanh paused in front of a water hole on the golf course, motioned for us to sit and meditate for 20 minutes, then rose and slowly began the snail's trek back.

Three days in silence. No networking. No idle conversation. Contemplation forced us to focus on the present moment, pay attention and become more aware. We were told to tell the truth about what we were holding inside – our feelings, judgments and thoughts.

I learned from this experience that silence is one of life's greatest teachers. Becoming aware and paying attention to the now is the key to surrendering to the process of life. With surrender – or letting go – we become calm and feel an inner peace that most people would give anything to have. It doesn't have to be difficult to find inner peace. You just have to ask for it and be willing to stay quiet long enough to attain it. And then do this over and over again until peace is your way of living.

Rx #30: You cannot allow others to rob you of your happiness.

Remaining balanced, especially in an aggravating situation is an art form. When we lose our equilibrium, we enter an insecure space where making rational decisions become difficult. The physical body wants to remain in homeostasis, a place where everything functions like clockwork. But stress tilts the scale, stops the clock, and interrupts its precise functioning.

While you can change some things by altering certain patterns of behavior, like learning to say no and not taking on too many obligations, you also need to accept the fact that certain things will not change. Customers frequently complain and bosses often demand more than you can produce. If you met a quota, it may then be set higher; deadlines may be moved up and more work heaped on you if you're efficient and organized.

One way to cope is to learn to let go both physically and emotionally. If you feel the need, go to the restroom and cry, or walk outside and scream or take deep breaths for 10 minutes. Move your body so that negative energy is released.

Refusing to engage in negative behavior when you are vulnerable is important. Though going home and eating a gallon of ice cream or drowning your aggravation in alcohol may give you temporary relief, it is also counterproductive. Instead, go for a brisk walk or some other form of exercise. The happy endorphin hormones will kick in and push out the stressful work residue inside you. Try to just let it pass through your system.

Focus on something positive or have a conversation with someone who'll be sympathetic. Don't let the negativity of others poison you and don't pass on that toxic mindset to the people you love and who love you. Let...It...Go.

Rx #31: Try not to attach emotional or mental baggage to events that are insignificant in the larger scheme of things. Let the past stay in the past and start each minute anew.

The Snowball Effect

Most large corporations see workers as a means to an end. Employees are expendable as long as profits rise and deadlines are met. The results can be disastrous for those who bear the emotional and physical burden of working for companies that do not care about their workers. Unfortunately, many are watching their investment portfolios and pensions disappear with the failings of large multi-national corporations and their short-sighted executive teams.

Years of corruption and unethical business behavior for the sake of bottom-line profits have caught up to a once financially strong and growing nation. We can only hope a new day is now dawning on Wall Street and in America that will result in companies that link the health of their workers to the success of their organization. This would be good news for many workers laboring for employers with little regard for their employees.

Until the trends shift to responsibility and accountability, employees are likely to grow increasingly intolerant of heavy workloads, insufficient breaks, extended hours, tight deadlines, and routine tasks that have little inherent meaning. These realities, added to escalating financial concerns, can lead to "survival" behavior in employees and resulting in loss of personal initiative and creativity.

It's important to remember that we all have a basic urge to be creative – whether it's cooking a meal; redesigning a microchip; painting a masterpiece; writing a book, a screenplay, a song; or simply finding shortcuts to make our work more efficient. We also have the basic need to be acknowledged for our achievements. Too often, the workplace does not provide the opportunity for approval and support that would foster any desire to be more productive. When management does not seek input from workers in decision – making processes and communication is poor, the workplace can become a stressful place rather than a comfortable exchange.

If you are an employer or manager, make the effort to provide opportunities for employee input and creativity. As an employee, ask your employers or supervisors if they are open to your ideas. If not, find a work environment that encourages and respects your individual talents and skills.

Bert, a 47-year-old married man with two daughters, lost the use of his left arm after an auto accident. A short time afterwards he had a stroke and his attention span was severely limited. As a result, Bert could no longer function in his old capacity and that made him anxious.

"I work in a family business, which puts a strain on my relationship with my parents," he told me. "Since I see them every day, the tension has become unbearable."

"How does that make you feel?" I asked.

"Awful"

"What can you do to change the situation?"

"Nothing – unless I quit – and who else would hire me now that I'm disabled?"

"Talk to them," I said. "Tell them you feel emasculated. Be honest and open. You have nothing to lose and everything to gain with your candor. If they sense your anguish, which they might because you are family, compassion will prevail and a resolution will come about. "Just remind yourself that you are physically challenged, not mentally, emotionally or spiritually disabled. You are the same person as before."

Bert took my advice. "You won't believe what happened," he told me. "Every member of the family was completely surprised when I expressed my feelings of inadequacy. They quickly pointed out all my contributions to the business and how I have helped. My perception has turned around 180 degrees. I see myself now for what I am bringing to the table rather than what I have lost due to the accident and stroke."

Rx 32: Only you can save yourself; no one can do it for you. You are the only one who can change a situation and actualize your dreams.

I learned this the hard way. I also learned that stuff happens. And so does magic. For magic to prevail, we must be in the flow. This means that we must live life like a leaf floating on a river effortlessly winding its way downstream past the unexpected twists and turns. The leaf does not struggle, but instead moves with ease around boulders and logs.

If we are in the state of flow, our journey will seem effortless. And we will be rewarded when unrelated events come together in time. This is called "synchronicity" or "serendipity." I learned a lot about flow by spending time with Allen Ginsberg, a Beat writer and the greatest American poet of our time. Ginsberg spent a lot of time chanting and reading his poetry. It was easy to see how passion and love for your craft can make a difference in your life. I saw that special quality in Ginsberg.

Following your passion and changing directions is not easy, but it is mandatory if you want to be happy and avoid stress. Living in the past can be deadly. We miss out on life entirely when we cling to the past.

Every breath we take is new and different. That's why it is important to be fully present in each minute riding each breath – knowing that change is inevitable.

There's nothing wrong with changing who you are or what you do. Each day people try new jobs, get into new situations, and lead different lifestyles. They quit high-paying jobs and go to mountaintops to contemplate their fate.

But one thing I know for sure is that the more we need to be something other than what we are, the further removed we become from living life in bliss. We need to listen to the deep inner voice inside ourselves that is calling out to us. It is easy to become clones of society, following contemporary templates.

When we do that we are led off a cliff away from our true being – and that is where stress originates.

I would say "Take a Risk – sky dive." Don't stagnate, or sit for years in a familiar situation that makes you comfortable but not happy. There are many lessons to learn in this dance of life when we open ourselves up to being fully present.

Marion's Story – the Good, the Bad and the Stress

Marion's boss Brian used intimidation and fear because it made him feel important. Although Marion was competent at her job, she didn't feel that way. Brian liked to brag that he could do her job with one hand tied behind his back. Marion lived in constant fear that he'd fire her. Then, one Monday morning, the day after she bought her daughter a new car, her worst fear materialized. He did fire her.

"I drove home in a trance," Marion recalled. "I simply didn't have a clue how I would manage the rent, tuition, car payments and my other expenses with no money coming in."

Some editors threw her freelance assignments, but there was no steady flow of income.

"In some ways it was a relief not to see Brian every day, but I traded in one kind of stress for another."

Rx #33: Imagine your worst fear, and then find a remedy before it happens. Know what you should do in advance so you can move into action quickly. Having a plan will immediately reduce your stress so you'll be ready for the emergency if one occurs.

It's important to be proactive, not only in your work but in all phases of your life. You should be in the NOW; experiencing life to the fullest at every moment, but that doesn't mean you can ignore the future. Be prepared with a Plan A and a Plan B. If your plans are in place, you won't have to play the victim waiting for the ax to fall.

Think about it this way: If you lived in a hurricane-prone area, you would keep water and emergency supplies available – just in case. If you lived in an area with earthquakes, you would be prepared to take action in a moment's notice. If you lived in Tornado Alley you would have a safe room and an emergency plan.

Everything requires a plan, and that comes from being in a place of calmness. Regardless of what catastrophe might occur, the remedy is being in a peaceful state so you can take the initiative to avert disaster. If you have the tools to remain calm and get through the worst of times, you have a survival kit.

Kate used all of her vacation time when her son came down with the chicken pox. Since chicken pox is highly contagious, no one wanted to baby-sit for her. Because of this, Kate did not get paid for an entire week.

Could Kate have planned for this emergency in advance? Yes, she could have reserved a few vacation or sick days, just in case her children got sick. She could have lined up a family member to baby-sit in case of an emergency. These options could have served as a viable Plan A and Plan B.

Rx #34: Unpleasant situations and toxic people cause anxieties. Some things cannot be changed, so change must come from within.

According to government studies, a healthy organization is defined as one that has low rates of illness, injury and disability. Some low-stress workplaces give time-management courses and have health clubs or gyms. They also offer counseling for employees with problems at home. Stress management training may reduce stress symptoms such as anxiety and sleep disturbances. However, these programs can have two major drawbacks: (1) The beneficial effect on stress symptoms is often short-lived; and (2) They ignore important root causes of stress because they focus on the worker and not the environment.

If you have to contend with nasty bosses, rude coworkers and a toxic work environment, you need to find a few minutes each day to do some of the exercises in this book. Do what time allows. Choose from any one of these exercises (you can find the page numbers on the Table of Contents, or visit my website www.stressreduction.com) for a complete list: The Two-Minute Break, Sitting Meditations, Climbing the Mountain Meditation, Workplace Visualization, Body Scan, and the Eyelid Meditation. You will experience a feeling of relief. Even if the exercise does not change your job or the people you interact with, you might have an "aha" moment during meditation that will give you the insight to fix your problems.

Learning Mindful Communication

I've counseled hundreds of people who want to change things about their workplace. The most common complaint revolves around communication. Here are a few common problems and steps to relieve the stress that it may cause.

(1) "No one really understands my needs and ideas." Instead of complaining, make two lists. One with your needs and one with your ideas. Then schedule a time to sit down with your supervisor to discuss them. You may also consider asking your supervisor where they could use additional help. Supervisors may be more open to meeting your needs if they see that you are sincerely interested in helping them meet theirs.

(2) "I'm left out of the loop." Communicate to your co-workers and superiors that you would like to be included in the decision-making process and that you have creative ideas to contribute. Then be ready to back up your statement when asked to sit in a meeting.

(3) "I'm not encouraged to share ideas." Ask around and find out if it is company policy not to volunteer ideas, or if you're just being kept out of the loop. Management may feel that "sharing" doesn't foster productivity, or perhaps they want to come up with all the ideas. If you prefer an environment where information is shared and staff communication is encouraged, it may be the time to look for another job.

(4) "No one talks to me as a person; I feel like a cog in a wheel." Chances are this is simply not the kind of job that will bring out the best in you.

If you like interpersonal relations, look for a job where you are asked to interact and offer ideas.

(5) "Nobody understands where I am coming from." Where are you coming from? If your values are not in sync with the company you're working for, either learn to adapt or move on and find another job.

(6) "There's a lack of communication between employees and management." I hate to tell you this, but that's the way it is in corporate America. There's a pecking order, and in most companies it's strictly adhered to. If this causes you anxiety and sleeplessness, you may be able to work your way up the corporate ladder to a position where you can make changes. But it might be better for your emotional well being to find a job that's more in alignment with your preferences.

(7) "The company sets unrealistic deadlines." There is really nothing you can do about this, but getting organized to meet deadlines is one way to handle it, or you can find a new job and move on.

(8) "MY supervisor doesn't back me up." This is tough because you cannot change other people; you can only change yourself. Once you know that you're going to be left flapping in the breeze, you have a hard decision to make: Stay and learn to cope, using some of the meditations in this book, or consider moving on.

Rx #35: Since conflict causes stress, you must find a way to deal with the situation without causing more stress on your system.

I learned this at the Naropa Institute in Boulder, Colorado, under the guidance and teachings of Chogyam Trungpa Rinpoche, where I studied contemplative psychotherapy, space awareness, Maitri training (loving kindness), and other forms of meditation.

Rinpoche's book, *Cutting Through Spiritual Materialism*, is a classic in this genre.

Rinpoche often said that the path to enlightenment is sitting in meditation and following the breath. He also advised us to watch the breath come and go.

I had been using a mantra (a group of words that, repeated over and over, bring peace and calm) since taking a Transcendental Meditation ™ course two years earlier and had practiced 20 minutes of meditation twice a day every day. The result is that it greatly reduced my stress and anxiety, lowered my blood pressure, and gave me a sense of calm along with increased energy.

Rx #36: There is no trick to meditating, but there is a reward. Total relaxation is your birthright. We all deserve to be at rest. And remember, a body that can find a place of rest wants to return to that place of rest.

After one of his talks about the merits of doing nothing more than watching the breath come and go, I walked to the edge of the stage and stated my case, saying that using a TM mantra was working for me so what should I do?

Chogyam Trungpa Rinpoche looked at me and said: "Follow the breath." I had noticed my resistance to this passive exercise. I tried and tried but it created more anxiety in me. So I had to learn to let go. I resumed my practice of focusing on a Sanskrit mantra with my eyes closed. The anxiety abated; calmness and peace returned to me afterwards.

This was a great lesson for me. I discovered that the path to inner peace and tranquility is already within every one of us, but that our paths will probably be different. That is why in this book I offer so many stress-relief exercises that lead to the same destination. Just trust your inner source and follow your intuition and your heart.

Managing Job Stress

When I was in Mexico conducting a stress reduction workshop, I received an e-mail from Ned, a 49-year-old CEO for a multi-million dollar healthcare company. Because of the company's business problems, Ned was experiencing anxiety and panic attacks.

"My anxiety has gotten so out of control that I woke my wife up with my restless sleeping," he told me when he arrived at my retreat. "I feel like I'm spiraling out of control."

The first things I taught him were meditation techniques and breathing exercises such as chi-kung, a form of healing movements to open blockages in his body. We met twice a day for several days, and after he returned home he called me.

"I meditated on the plane and was so full of energy that my wife asked if I had met someone while I was away," he told me, laughing. He continued to improve, sticking to the lifestyle program he learned during his stay with me. A month later, he called to ask about setting up a three-day program for his top 10 employees. He wanted them to learn the same meditation techniques I taught him to calm his anxieties.

Ned called again several months later. Most of these top employees had formed a chi kung class. The group meets three times a week during work hours (Ned's suggestion) in the company's atrium. Ned attends the classes with his staff when he can and said that his commitment and interest in their welfare has made a huge difference in their level of productivity and overall happiness. "My interaction with them is creating bonds that didn't exist before," he said. "It's very rewarding for all of us."

I strongly encourage the daily meditations in this book to help drain away stress. See my website www.stressreduction.com for available CD's and DVD's. Even if you cannot attend one of my seminars, there are numerous ways that you can take the edge off stress while at work:

- ➢ Whenever possible, get up and walk. Stroll down the halls or around the building. If you work at home, go out for fresh air. Fold laundry; stare out the window for a few minutes. Give your mind a rest.

- ➢ If you're in an office, try clenching and unclenching your fists. Do this ten times and repeat a mantra to help relieve stress. It can be something as commonly used as "Om," which is considered the universal vibration to promote calmness.

- ➢ Eating crunchy foods helps unclench the jaw. Try carrots, celery sticks or rice cakes. They relax tightened muscles and provide nutrition at the same time.

- ➢ Breathe in through the nose and let the air out through the mouth. Keep your teeth together and make a hissing sound. Do this three times, ignoring the strange looks your co-workers give you.

- ➢ After work, get to a body of water – ocean, lake, pool or bathtub – and take a large gulp of air, then put your head

under water and blow it out with a scream. This releases
negative energy and toxins in the body.

> Know that nothing lasts forever – jobs, bosses and co-workers
> come and go. If you can stick it out, there will be relief down
> the road. If you absolutely cannot continue working where
> you are, then you have an opportunity to find a new job or
> career.

I have an exercise that you can use to temporarily relieve stress during
the day. THE NINE DOTS calls for patience and concentration and will
take your mind off your troubles for awhile. Connect these nine dots
with four straight lines, without lifting the pencil and without retracing
any of the lines (See page 213 for the solution).

     .   .   .

     .   .   .

     .   .   .

Now let's get back to the story of Marion and her difficult boss.

Marion, who was unemployed, sat at a window at home
staring into space, racking her brain for something she could do. She
couldn't find a job at the local newspaper, so she started her own
business designing a program to teach business writing to corporate
employees.

"I think managers will hire me for lunchtime seminars," she told me. I've had pamphlets and business cards printed, and I have a fifty-page syllabus."

I congratulated her for having such a great plan, but before she could implement it a former colleague quit and she was called back to her old job.

"It was a gut-wrenching decision," she said. "On one hand, I needed the steady paycheck, but I knew I was going back to hell." Once again her anxiety escalated, but this time she had a different attitude: The worst case scenario had already happened and she had survived, so Brian no longer had the negative effect on her that he once had. She now had a Plan A, which was a mantra I had given her. She put it on her computer and every time Brian walked by her, or whenever she felt anxious, she repeated it.

She worked with Brian for two years. She was able to handle it because she put her energy into meditation, breathing exercises, stress-reduction clinics and spiritual work. Then Brian was fired and the entire department was relieved. The new boss, Ray, was cheerful and appreciative. Ray let everyone do their work without interfering like Brian did. He knew they were all professionals who could deliver their work on time. It's been nine years since Brian left and Marion is still working at the same job – with Ray.

Rx #37: You cannot change others, so learn to accept them. Stay in the moment and know that everything is alright now.

Do you love your job and feel rewarded, or is it just the opposite? As you read these questions, think about how your job makes you feel.

1. Does it negatively affect your emotions and your mental well-being?

2. Is it mildly stressful; does the stress ebb and flow at a reasonable pace?

3. Are the stressors short-term or long-term – like struggling to fill constant quotas or meet unreasonable deadlines?

4. Are you creating your own stress by imagining what might go wrong?

5. Are you in a no-win situation?

6. Would you be better off cutting your losses, taking a possible cut in pay, and landing a job you might really love?

Stress isn't only in the corporate world. It's pervasive in school systems from pre-K through the university level. Students live in a constant state of high anxiety with tests, exams, homework assignments and peer pressure. Teachers have to deal with students, colleagues and administrative faculty. At some levels, they also must deal with the "publish or perish" dictum that means their work must be seen in trade or educational journals.

Ashley, a 37-year-old schoolteacher, started out with enthusiasm and optimism. "I wanted to make a difference by helping kids with learning disabilities." She said to me. "Now I feel as though I wasted fourteen years of my life."

She began teaching children but after a few years she was so stressed out that she decided to work with older students.

Unfortunately, she wound up in a small department with staff members who gossiped, complained, and bullied her.

The strong fluorescent lights gave her migraine headaches. The school was filthy and a health hazard. Kids spit on the floor. Police visited the place regularly to handle disturbances, which caused physical pain throughout her body. Although there were some talented kids and staff members she liked, Ashley summed up the job as "a polluted swamp of rules, schedules and administrative politics."

Like so many other people, Ashley had become a slave to her paycheck. Although she tried to ignore the ugliness of her surroundings, the stress of the situation drained her happiness and made her extremely depressed.

"I started teaching because I loved little kids and wanted to support them, especially in ways I didn't get growing up," she said. "But I found myself yearning for a soul connection and heart space that didn't exist in the classroom. Any satisfaction I got from helping students was offset by the horrible work environment. Now I know why so many staff members came in hung over. Others were sick or depressed. Two members of the department were undermining the whole department, and the principal was blind to it. Plus, there was a lot of turnover.

"My immune system went down and I had congestion in my lungs," she says. "I was anxious all the time and dreaded going to work, so I took an extended medical leave. I guess I'm lucky, because I took my life back after I left."

Ashlee was angry at herself for having spent so much time in a toxic environment and left without long-term financial benefits. She felt she had wasted a good portion of her adult life, which added to her frustration and unhappiness. Because of this, her health suffered and she became a slave to the stress in her system.

Rx #38: There is no reason to give someone else the power to determine whether you are going to have a good day or a bad day.

In any work situation there is a potential for conflict with co-workers. You never know who might gossip about you behind your back and in any office there will be someone who grates on your nerves. Maybe they clip their nails at their desk, laugh uncontrollably, talk non-stop or too loudly, or take your newspaper before you've finished reading it. Some may yell; others could be mean-spirited or difficult to get along with. That can make your blood boil and give you a pounding headache. That's why you'll never know when someone will turn an otherwise happy office into a miserable workplace – causing you and others a lot of stress.

Often these difficult people have not learned Mindful Communication and are not acting reasonably. Perhaps they are bringing a bucket of emotional baggage and heartache to work and are unknowingly taking it out on others. They make their problem your problem, and while it's not fair, there's usually not much you can do about it. Do you know what you have to do? You have to change YOUR feelings and attitudes about them and the situation.

Rx #39: No matter how competent and wonderful you are, it's impossible to please everybody. So stop trying. Do your job and let other people's nastiness roll off your back.

The best way to deal with a negative situation is to see it coming. If you're going to have to work closely with a toxic coworker, know ahead of time how you're going to handle the situation. Be aware of your limitations and your options. Embrace your self-confidence and hold steady to your happiness – that way they will be unable to upset you.

Rx #40: Recognize that the other people's problems are theirs. Don't make them yours and don't take them personally.

People who thrive on being difficult and cause unnecessary tension also thrive on controversy. Any exchange of negative words makes them feel powerful and fuels their need for conflict. So be cheerful in the face of adversity; in other words, "kill them with kindness." They will become either too frustrated or too bored to continue their harassment. This is a tai chi application called "ward off and neutralize."

This played out in full force when I met Tennessee Williams in Key West, Florida. I had been hired for three days to help film a segment on Fantasy Fest for HBO. The parade was a main event at this initiation of Fantasy Fest, and Williams was to be one of the judges on the reviewing stand.

Shortly into filming, one of our helpers came rushing through the crowd insisting that we hurry to the reviewing stand because Williams was drunk and almost ready to pass out. We pushed our way through the crowd and ran up the reviewing ramp as we watched him nodding back and forth. I thrust the microphone under his bobbing face and asked, "Mr. Williams – what do you think of Halloween?" He replied, "Halloween...is...a...drag," and passed out at the reviewing table.

This incident was a powerful reminder that some of the most successful accomplished celebrities and intellectuals are human – perhaps even as unhappy – as the homeless person on the street.

Rx #41: A smile, a compliment and a kind word goes a long way in making a less stressful work environment. A positive attitude diffuses negativity and cuts through toxic pollution.

Some difficult people are filled with pent-up frustration and simply need an ally or a person who will listen. By offering a sympathetic ear, you may be able to ease the situation between you and the agitated worker. Just remember that anything told in confidence remains confidential.

Rx #42: Don't gossip or spread rumors. Keep confidential information to yourself. Respect the privacy of others. Remember: Great minds discuss ideas, mediocre minds discuss events, and small minds discuss people.

Difficult people are able to create a hostile work atmosphere, and that in itself can lower productivity by making it hard to concentrate. Complaining to the boss can be counterproductive and might lead to you being fired. If you're stuck dealing with obnoxious, loud, or toxic coworkers and it is beginning to affect your health and outlook on life, it may be time to cut your losses and find new work.

Rx #43: Believe it or not, getting fired or leaving a job because of stress usually turns out to be a blessing in disguise.

Office politics are part of most workplace environments. Workers who pursue their personal hidden agendas at the expense of others are people to either avoid or learn to have compassion for. It will bother you less if you learn how the political game is played in your office and refuse to be sucked in by it.

Rx #44: Know how office politics can affect you. Learn who has power and clout and make nice – or at least stay under their radar.

Jumping to conclusions is easy, but when we interpret other people's actions we often assume the worst without knowing the facts. Then, too often, we compound our stress by talking to our colleagues who can spread rumors with no basis in reality.

Rx #45: Refrain from speaking or acting before hearing all the facts. Stop wasting your time and energy on what you think may have happened. There may be a perfectly good explanation for a particular action. Ask for it.

Double-talk involves the deliberate use of ambiguous, vague or confusing language spoken or written in a sincere or meaningful tone. Some managers are masters of this. It's a subversive way of being able to shift the blame when things go wrong. When you hear double-talk, try to discover motives, hidden agendas and their intention by listening carefully and objectively.

Rx #47: No one can make you feel a certain way. You have the power to respond, so don't give that power away. Keep in mind that YOU are in charge of your emotions, and YOU determine the amount of stress you experience in your life.

Breathing to Nirvana – The Meditation Story

Imagine dropping a pebble into a well. Pretty soon a ripple effect will take place and waves will move outward. If you stay centered in your true self – free from anxiety – then you will be able to maintain your integrity and autonomy.

One way to avoid being touched by the ripples of everyday life (stress, anxiety and depression) is to meditate. It is your breath and your ability to go under the waves of everyday life that makes the difference between a happy life and miserable one. Which one do you want?

If we concentrate – and stay quiet – we can feel the movement of our breath. We can experience the gentle expansion of our breath, receding as it goes out – like riding a wave. Because our bodies are made mostly of water, it is easy to feel this movement.

As you focus on the breath, you are anchored in the solar plexus. You are distanced from the chattering minds. There is no right way or wrong way of meditating. Watch your breath come in and go out, just as it does every moment of the day. By doing so, you are creating an awareness of what is happening in your being. If the breath seems to move around, that's OK, and if your mind wanders, that's fine too. Just redirect your attention and focus back to the breath. Without rejecting or pursuing them, notice the sensations in the body and the thoughts on your mind. See if you can establish a primary connection with the breath in this moment, and see if you can simultaneously observe your body sensations.

You are giving yourself over to wakefulness. Allow the breath to be center stage. Is the mind still with the breath? What are your thoughts, emotions, impulses and perceptions? Can you be here fully? Can you be in your body right now as it is? Can you be simply awake, not trying to get anywhere?

Be here now, realizing that your life is unfolding in this very breath.

Working with the Flow

You can swim upstream, fighting the tide, feeling unfulfilled, unhappy and stressed to the max. Or you can find something you love doing – a job that's in sync with your talent, your personality, your heart and your zest for life. It's never too early or too late to find something that turns you on or energizes you. When that happens, you can't wait to jump out of bed in the morning and get to work. When was the last time you felt that way?

Chad was eager to be independent and on his own when he started working part-time at age 14. He preferred having his own money rather than relying on his parents for an allowance. He came to see me when he was only 16, complaining of shortness of breath, nausea, heart palpitations and a general feeling of anxiety.

"It's stress," I told him. "And you're much too young to be this stressed out."

When I met Norman Mailer, the world-famous author, he told me about writing. "The only way to write," he said, "is to write." I thought about his pragmatic notion about this creative craft and realized that he was right. You have to go with the flow – even if it is solely a creative one – until you find the right rhythm.

I also realized that we are all the same – whether we have an asterisk under our name or a marquee that announces our performance to the world. I found out that celebrities were often doing something they truly liked, rather than following the herd.

This willingness to march to the beat of their own drummer gave me respect for them, rather than inspiring awe. That's why it was natural for me to rub shoulders with so many celebrities throughout my career. That also meant going with the flow, whether it was with someone famous or not.

On three different occasions, I worked as an extra on the popular television series "Miami Vice" and had conversations with actor Don Johnson. My sailboat was the backdrop at Miami Marina for the last show in the series and Don Johnson's boat was parked directly across from mine. Being on a movie set is, as they say, like watching grass grow. Unless you have speaking lines and are a Screen Actors Guild member, the job pays very little. But you do it for the fun (and the flow).

The last time I saw Johnson he was standing alone in front of my boat, so I took the occasion to engage him in conversation. Johnson told me that he was afraid of the alligator that was seen chained in the boat's cockpit. On one of the first episodes it lunged at him and came too close for comfort before the chain jerked it to a stop. This is real stress, but Johnson was able to go with the flow. He learned that trick by working as an actor where what is real is not and what is unreal could very well become real.

As a non-speaking body double in the filming of "Leopold Bloom," I also met actor/playwright Sam Shepherd, a man who really knows how to go with the flow. We had a pleasant conversation about Charleston, South Carolina where the movie was filmed and talked about what he did in his down time. Later I had a similar conversation with Dennis Hopper. These were actors who had attained fame, yet they were not overly impressed with themselves. That in itself can lead to a better life than trying to become someone you are not or someone others want you to be.

Rx #48: We can take personal responsibility and create an exciting and dynamic life instead of staying in a miserable situation and making ourselves sick. Regardless of our chronological age, we have free will. This is our birthright.

You might think you are stuck in a situation like Chad's with an unfulfilling job that offers no sense of self-worth and no future. You might have a boss who's a jerk and causes you to bite your tongue and put up with office politics. As we've already discussed, bottling up anger and frustration is not healthy, but neither is complaining. Resist the temptation to talk with your colleagues about how awful the boss is and how intimidating the work conditions are. The reason? There's a snitch in every bunch. If he or she finds out, I can guarantee that your life will be even more stressful. Resist the urge to speak negatively about anyone.

Rx #49: Listen to your heart as well as your body. What your gut tells you to do is always correct. Be willing to leave toxic work situations before they create illness. Life is too short, so why use it up in a work environment that makes you unhappy or sick? Remember, you have free will.

Here are a few things you can try to help reduce stress and perhaps help you enjoy the time you spend on the job:

➢ *Stay in integrity.* It's in your best self-interest to continue doing your job and doing it well. Stay focused and be productive. If you do a good job and an opportunity for advancement arises, you may be able to move into a better position with a bigger paycheck. This won't make your boss a nicer person, but at least you'll be better compensated for your talents.

> *Make an effort to understand your boss's management style and adapt to it.* If he's a micromanager, give him constant updates and details on what you're doing, even if you think it's pointless and a waste of time.

> *Effective communication is very important and it works both ways.* If your boss is unclear in what he or she wants you to do, ask questions until you know what's expected. During performance evaluations, ask what you can do to meet his or her expectations.

Leaving a job is a last resort, especially if you like your work and its benefits, co-workers and company culture. But you should consider your health – and the health of your loved ones. It is important to weigh your options, and if you decide that leaving is the best option, do it right. Don't yell "I quit!" Don't burn your bridges or insult your boss. Instead, be proactive by updating your resume, networking, looking for another job and going on interviews. The goal is to have another job lined up before you tell your boss you're leaving. Always leave on good terms, because you never know what the future holds. You might need a letter of recommendation someday.

Those who are self-employed face a different set of problems. They might not have a difficult boss or need to contend with office politics, but the pressure is on them 24/7. Self-employed people often scramble for work and find it's either feast or famine. Their paychecks might be irregular, and they have a lot more responsibility for every aspect of the business. The self-employed often find themselves overwhelmed, having taken on too many projects.

Marcos, a 28-year old advertising executive, learned early on that he was not suited for the corporate world. Despite his talent and easygoing personality, he felt restricted in his creative expression. Working at the advertising/public relations agency had its creative side, but when he was assigned a mundane task and trapped at his desk he experienced great anxiety. These anxious moments flooded his body with cortisol and epinephrine, creating a constant state of agitation.

On several occasions, Marcos experienced panic attacks when he was driving to meetings with his boss. When that happened he had to ask the boss to pull the car over so he could use the bathroom to de-stress. His hands trembled and his heart felt as though it would leap out of his chest.

Because he had a wife and two children depending on him financially and emotionally, Marcos knew he was in a treacherous position.

Like Marcos, many people find themselves stuck in a job they don't enjoy. The stress of being in a work situation like this can cause a stroke, heart attack, nervous breakdown, alcoholism or drug addiction.

During our sessions, I learned that Marcos' workplace anxiety started when he was a teen and continued to plague him from job to job. He thought it would be different every time, but his panic attacks resurfaced at every job and each time Marcos would sabotage his work relationships as a result. After he quit or was fired, his primary anxiety level would vanish only to be replaced with feelings of guilt, failure and, soon, more anxiety.

"I should have been able to control my anxiety," he told me. "Why can't I be normal?"

While anxiety disorder is widely recognized today, it continues to torment those who experience it. Drugs and psychotherapy aren't always the perfect answer. I discovered that Marcos, his father and his paternal grandmother all suffered from anxiety. Since it was considered a weakness rather than a disorder in those days, they managed to camouflage their physical, mental, and emotional hell. Marcos' anxiety was his inheritance, and counseling and tranquilizers didn't control his workplace attacks.

When someone like Marcos comes to my office, I look at the whole person. Rather than seeing Marcos' problem as simply related to his work, I saw it as only part of his issues. Eager to get off the treadmill that kept him repeating his destructive pattern, Marcos learned meditation techniques to quiet his mind. It was then that he arrived at the realization that self-employment would give him control over his environment and reduce his workplace anxiety.

He started out using his media talent and parlayed it into a consulting business. With his photography and writing skills, he learned technology and computer skills at a community college so he could market himself on the web.

We worked together on lifestyle changes, including an exercise routine, daily sitting meditation practice, nutrition and chi kung. This put him in a place of calmness and equanimity that increased his energy and creative level.

Self-employment is not always the perfect solution to this problem. Lack of a steady paycheck can cause tension and anxiety for some people. However, the choice is yours. Regardless of the outcome, decide what feels best for you. Meditation and lifestyle changes can help you to make the right choice. For Marcos the decision to become self-employed was a positive change. He didn't earn the salary he did in the past, but he lived a relaxed and happy life instead.

Rx #50: The choice to work for others or to be self-employed is yours to make. Weigh the pros and cons of both – then trust in yourself. You can succeed in anything you choose if you have a dream and the desire to do so.

Love is a Many Splendored Thing – But Not in the Office

Office romances are always a minefield of potential stress and chaos. An office romance will likely, sooner or later, intensify the stress in your life. In the long run it may cost you your job or a client. No matter how valuable you think you are, or how much your romantic partner loves you, it will usually result in a grave amount of stress. So think long and hard before you let your heart rule your head.

The Stress-Free Workspace – Meditation Mode

When you're stuck in a job and your stress starts to build, there is a quick and simple getaway that will help. Go on a mental mini-vacation and no one else will know where you are or that you have gone anywhere.

If I asked you to tell me about your favorite place to relax, a place where you feel peaceful, calm and safe, what would be your answer? For me it's the beach.

sis
66 Hippocrates Way
st Palm Beach, FL
A
411

1-471-5867

| erchant #: | 364331 |
| avoice #: | 9001094813 |

us. type:	Spa
olio #:	706951
taff #:	8912

| /28/2020 | 11:26:05 |

| ard #: | ************1416 |
| ard type: | MasterCard |

| ransaction: | Purchase |
| otal: | 160.40 |

| ut. #: | 002816003237 |
| Reference #: | 86069T |

*** Purchase - Success ***

2020-01-28 11:26:07 86069T

_____
Signature

Cardholder will pay card issuer above
amount pursuant to Cardholder Agreement.

Client Copy

This is your workplace visualization. Try it now. Close your eyes and take yourself to that spot in your mind.

This exercise doesn't take long and requires only mental transportation (best part – no reservations or tickets). Two minutes visiting your favorite spot will release comforting hormones to reduce work stress and nourish your brain and your body.

Chapter 5

RELEASING STRESS CREATORS

"By letting go it all gets done. The world is won by those who let it go. But when you try and try, the world is beyond the winning." – Lao Tzu

A quiz: HOW TIGHT ARE YOU CLINGING?

What holds you back from truly experiencing life is the fear we call the "what if." How tightly do you cling to your current lifestyle and relationships simply because you are afraid to make a new move?

Take this quiz to get a glimpse of how stuck you are. Consider the questions using the criteria of a scale from one to five. Five being very often, one being never.

5-very often **4**-often **3**-sometimes **2**-infrequently **1**-rarely or never

1. I don't like change.   _____
2. I am comforted by my possessions. _____
3. My closet is stuffed with things I don't wear. _____
4. I have a stack of unopened bills. _____
5. It's hard for me to throw away food. _____
6. I dwell on souvenirs and photos of old lovers; they remind me of the good times. _____
7. I like clutter. _____

8. My job stinks. _____
9. I don't enjoy my relationship with my significant other.

    _____
10. I hate to be alone. _____

Notice that I didn't ask for true or false, yes or no. I am asking instead for you to consider the degree to which you may be denying yourself the joys of life. If you believe any of these are true, then you're clinging to the past and fearful of moving on. I won't say let go, but I will give you some techniques in this chapter that might help you change the way you see things.

Sensing Your Own Future

The first and most important act is to accept your limitations and not be paralyzed by your fear. You can transform your spirit and reclaim the real you when you are ready.

Stop putting additional pressure on yourself to be somebody you're not. And stop trying to make a change you're not ready for. Transformations are subtle and have a logical time sequence. They happen over time. If you are open to new vistas (and a new stress-free life), then it will happen. Here are some things to consider.

➤ If you are restless, annoyed or irritated, allow yourself to BE.

➤ Accept yourself as you are without self-criticism.

➤ Let go of wanting things to be different. They are what they are for now until they change, either through circumstance or your own efforts.

➤ Let change come to you by placing yourself in a calm setting.

➤ There is no right or wrong way to feel.

➤ Whatever happens in your life is OK. You will deal with it by staying focused on the present (it is a "present," after all).

➤ Give yourself permission to observe the wonders of the universe without feeling that you are wasting time.

There's a little voice inside each of us. You can call it ESP, a sixth sense, conscience or intuition, but it knows all. It can predict the future and offer astonishingly accurate insights into the situations, people and relationships. This voice, called your "gut" or "gut feelings," is an innate form of wisdom that is your birthright. It's been described as a judgment that comes quickly into one's consciousness.

You might not know why you have a particular gut feeling, but it is often strong enough to make you act upon it. It's not a calculated decision, nor is it considered a rational thought. However, this little voice can save you a lot of grief, if only you would listen. The problem is that we tend to ignore this voice and go our merry way until trouble rears its head.

Brenda came to one of my stress-reduction classes because of a job related problem. She was dating a guy named Marty, whom she met while playing tennis. He was handsome and smart and a great Scrabble player; they really enjoyed their time together.

Marty had a standing Friday night date with Brenda because he told her he had to work every Saturday. Brenda accepted this weekend arrangement at face value and was OK with it.

One of the meditations I use is called the Body Scan. I have my clients lie on a mat and begin a relaxation that starts with the feet and works up to the top of the head. When Brenda did this exercise, she experienced tremendous feelings of conflict.

"I had the awful feeling that Marty was cheating on me," she said. "I could hear your voice and I tried to follow the meditation, but I couldn't relax because another voice was coming through loud and clear from somewhere deep inside me. It told me that he was dating someone else."

Brenda drove home from the class in a daze and when she walked in the door, she picked up the phone, called Marty and ended their relationship. He was stunned. But she remained steadfast despite his protest that she was the only one he was dating.

A few weeks later, feeling remorseful, Brenda called Marty to chat. "I thought maybe I'd made a mistake," she told me. "Maybe I acted too hastily. Maybe my gut feeling was wrong."

But later, she found out from a friend that Marty had been cheating on her. Her intuition had been right on target.

The point I'm making here is that Brenda was willing to say goodbye to Marty based entirely on the little voice that told her he was cheating. She had no evidence that he had someone else – only a gut instinct. And the best part is that she trusted and followed her intuition, which was accurate.

You may be searching for a deeper meaning in your life, or you may feel bogged down in the quicksand of life – obstacles, stress and unhealthy relationships. You may also find that taking control of your life is difficult or near impossible, and you may feel overwhelmed.

By listening to your body and your heart (yes that little voice) you are empowering yourself. With this new sense of strength you will be able to respond properly, minimizing your anxiety. But it takes mindfulness on your part.

Sometimes you have to let go of people you love because they are the ones who add to your stress. They can be parents, siblings, friends, children, lovers or spouse.

Russ, a 30-year-old artist came to see me because he was experiencing debilitating migraine headaches. Even though his passion for relaxation was sailing on weekends, he still developed migraines.

"Who goes sailing with you?" I asked.

"My wife and in-laws," he said.

"How do you get along with them?"

He paused and answered, "We get along well, but they've always been critical of my chosen lifestyle as an artist and they're on my case all the time about getting a real job."

Suddenly Russ grew quiet. He had what we call an "aha" experience. "I get it," he said. "I've been associating failure with fun; while I love sailing, my unconscious mind dreads hearing criticism."

Russ was able to tell his wife (who was very understanding) how he felt. So instead of sailing, they chose other social occasions to be with her parents. Now Russ is much more relaxed and he and his wife renamed his boat *Destination Relaxation.* Without his in-laws aboard his migraines disappeared and the joy he experienced while sailing returned.

It's not realistic for me to suggest that you let go of your relationships, but it is my mission to find out if a toxic situation or person is doing you harm. If so, would you be better off letting that situation or person go?

Rx #51: If there is a toxic situation or person who is a problem, you might want to consider cutting the ties and releasing the stress it's causing.

Letting go is the most natural thing you can do – and it's also one of the most difficult. Trees have no problem letting ripe fruit drop to the ground. In the wild, animals release their offspring into the world when it's time. Yet humans cling to possessions and relationships long after they have stopped being meaningful, joyous or fulfilling.

When you turn your back on obsessive thoughts, regret, anxiety, bitterness and toxic emotions, you free yourself to move forward with your life. You allow yourself the right to find joy. The ability to abandon the part of you that is unhappy – the part of you that is suffering – comes from that inner voice, the one that knows all.

Your gut instinct is not confused with contradictions about what you should or shouldn't do, or who you should or shouldn't be with. It knows what's best for you. So listen to it. Once you trust that your inner spirit knows what is best for you, the rest will take care of itself.

To help you see the truth, here is a little exercise I call "The Eyelid Meditation." It illustrates the powerful mind/body connection.

The Eyelid Meditation

Sit in a comfortable chair. Take your palms and put them over your ears so the fingertips meet at the top of your head. That's the crown. Now visualize a string pulling it up to the moon. When you do this, your spine will be drawn upward and your feet will be anchored to the floor. When you do this you will be connected to the Earth and to the Universe.

Now hold your palms in your lap and sense an alignment of your body. Take a deep breath and hold it, then let go. Repeat the breath, but on the exhale, allow your eyelids to close.

Bring your attention to your eyelids and release the tiny muscles in your eyes. If you allow them to relax, your eyes will feel heavy. Hold the feeling and let it go. If you are truly relaxed, your eyes will remain shut. Stay this way for a few moments then slowly open them.

You can do this exercise anywhere. The point is that letting go of tension is your choice. It's a conscious decision. You can open your eyes or you can remain relaxed. It's your choice.

Rx #52: You can cling to your tension, or you can release it. It's up to you whether to be stressed or relaxed.

Edwin's story – Letting Go

Letting go is great advice, but advice is cheap. The term "letting go" is so overused that if often seems as worthless as an old penny. But if you truly and genuinely want to learn the art of letting go, it will empower you.

In the summer of 2001 I was visiting a friend in Charleston, South Carolina. At the time I was offered a consulting job to establish a Mind/Body Center for a hospital group. The timing was perfect, so I decided to stay.

The study was terminated – unfortunately, at a time when it was most needed – because of the September 11 attack on the World Trade Center, but I chose to stay in Charleston because my daughter lived there. I liked the friendly atmosphere of this genteel southern city, so I opened a holistic psychotherapy practice there.

Business was slow, and the attendance at my stress reduction workshops was not stellar. A brief romance ended, and I was bored living in a small beach cottage on Sullivan's Island, quaint as it was.

Reflecting on the shortness of life – and living in the moment – I decided to let go. The epiphany I experienced was clear and specific. There was no getting around it – I had to surrender to the unlimited possibilities I faced.

In the poignant moment of letting go, my life changed. I was FREE. All those fearful thoughts about living, dying, making money and feeling guilty vanished on the spot. I knew I was OK. I was more than OK. I was ALIVE and living in the moment.

When I relinquished my control, I set myself free. That freedom gave me the strength to make calls to find people that could help me chart my future.

Rx #53: Letting go means giving up fear, control, old habits, guilt, regrets and voices from the past. It means living in the present.

After her divorce, L.A., who helped edit this book, left New York in 1986 with her nine-year-old daughter to make a new life in Florida. She had no alimony or child support, no place to live and no job prospects. She drove 1,400 miles to a strange place armed only with the knowledge that she would somehow make it work. Today, her daughter is happily married and L.A. makes a very good living as a freelance writer. She trusted her gut and she believed in herself.

I also learned a great deal about letting go from the great Beat poet Allen Ginsberg. In the summer of 1976, I was a guest professor at Rollins College in Winter Park, Florida, teaching "Literature of the

Beat Generation." As part of the Allen Ginsberg lecture, I arranged for a conference call with Ginsberg at the evening class.

Allen phoned me just prior to our class section to apologize saying his father, Louis, was on his deathbed and he would be enroute to New York City. "What would you like for me to tell the class?" I asked, thinking he might have some words of wisdom or a pithy comment. "Tell them it really doesn't matter, they're all going to die anyway."

So I wrote this quote on the chalk board with Ginsberg's name and date. While his comment was abrupt, it wasn't intended to be mean-spirited. Rather, he was putting life and death into perspective. He did not want us to sweat the small stuff. His father was dying and Allen was rushing to his bedside.

Ginsberg was living in the moment, not in the future or the past. This is where we should be at all times – that way we remain centered in the heart and able to live life to its fullest. In order to eliminate stress and make happiness our constant companion we need to be alive and honest – real and deliberate. And listening to Ginsberg that day I realized that he was a living embodiment of this healthy state of being. We should all try to do that, regardless of what others say about our thinking. Because in the end if we don't please ourselves, what good are we?

Rx #54: It takes a leap of faith and a positive can-do attitude to jump off the cliff and know you'll land on your feet. Only fear holds you back.

The Monkey Mind Effect

It's said that we have 50,000 thoughts per day. Most of them are not new. We rehash our feelings from the past and our fears and anxieties about the future over and over. We are rarely in the present.

After deciding to leave South Carolina and strike out for parts unknown, my head was filled with nonstop chatter, or what I call Monkey Mind. Much of it was drivel – meaningless thoughts about the past and fantasies about the future. This went on for weeks, interrupting important decisions I had to make. Even with all my years of experience, I was everywhere but in the present. I worried constantly and that only added to my anxiety.

While I was trying to decide where to move, I had a brief encounter with a couple I'd met in Puerto Escondido. Patricia had been a cultural anthropologist at the University of Mexico. Alejandro was an industrial engineer. They both took a leap of faith, leaving lucrative positions to open a healing center in a tiny fishing village on the Pacific coast of Mexico. Both of them were dedicated to meditation and the healing arts, and enjoying their new lifestyle.

When I got in touch with Patricia, I asked her if she needed someone with my skills – a doctorate in mind/body medicine, and experience in tai chi and chi kung.

She promptly got back to me and told me they couldn't afford to pay me. "It's not about the money," I responded. "I'm looking for shelter, food and a small income, just enough to cover my expenses."

Graciously, she offered a place for me to stay, even though we were practically strangers. I got on a plane and went to another country where I did not even know the language. I trusted that this was the place I needed to be. I truly let go in every sense of the word.

Rx #55: Worry adds to stress. It makes you crazy over something that may never happen.

Rx #56: Worry is like a bag of bricks. You can put it down at any time.

I learned this from renowned science-fiction writer Isaac Asimov. Asimov had an anxiety attack when we were aboard a ship leaving Cape Canaveral. Hugh Downs and Norman Mailer also got a case of cabin fever on board the "Mission Beyond Apollo" ship as we waited for the night launch of Apollo 17 and a few days of cruising to St. Thomas. I knew at the time that Asimov could easily have helped himself calm down if he knew how to meditate or think about something pleasant. Instead he let his angst get the better of him.

I also recall Downs' sense of urgency and his resulting coping mechanism. Once he learned that we were anchored in a restricted zone, he channeled his energy toward preparing for the night launch, volunteering to announce the countdown from the ships bridge. This was a way for him to distract himself from the discomfort he was experiencing at the moment.

When we confront our fears, rather than run away from them, they generally seem less threatening, like the boogeyman that appeared in the dark and disappeared by daylight when we were children. If we fill ourselves with light through relaxation techniques such as meditation, our adult boogeyman will disappear and be replaced with calm and peace.

In order to make the body and mind whole, you must uncover the guilt and melancholy that keeps you rooted in the past. Like an archaeologist, you need to find the site first, mark it, and then start chipping away at each layer that prevents you from finding the treasure. When you get there, the real YOU is revealed. Clinging to the past produces a chain of anxiety and stress that must be broken.

Peaceful Endings

Beverly was married to Nick for twelve years, a second marriage for each. Then Nick developed a brain tumor and their lives were in turmoil. When Beverly could no longer care for Nick, she reluctantly put him in a hospice facility where he died peacefully a few months later.

Beverly donated all of Nick's clothing to charity, but she kept three shirts in a drawer. She simply couldn't bear to throw them away. Then, one day while cleaning, she pulled out the shirts and studied them for a long time.

"They weren't taking up much space," She told me. "I knew they couldn't bring Nick back and I wanted to get rid of them."

"Why don't you? I asked.

She thought a long while before answering. "I feel guilty."

"If the shirts don't take up a lot of room, then keeping them shouldn't be a problem," I suggested. "But what I'm hearing is that you want to let them go."

Beverly nodded. "I have a lot of pictures of us together and scrapbooks of our good times. But I feel these three shirts are keeping me rooted in the past, like a silent link to Nick."

"It's hard to give away things that remind us of good times, as long as they don't put you in a state of depression of stress. You'll always have your memories of good times together," I told her.

Beverly nodded. A few hours later she called to say that she had donated the shirts to the thrift shop. Afterwards she felt as if a huge weight had been lifted from her shoulders.

Control Issues – Who is in Charge?

As you read the chapter on eating, when Francine took control of the clutter she began taking control of her life. So start with the physical things that you're clinging to. Let them go by doing these simple exercises.

➢ Pack up clothing that is out of fashion, too small or too big, or that you haven't worn in a year and donate them to charity.

➢ Get rid of souvenirs and stuffed animals that are collecting dust. Now go to your office or desk. Throw away useless bills or paperwork.

➢ Go into the kitchen and load up a carton of plates, bowls, glasses, and silverware that you don't use.

➢ Get rid of household knick-knacks that you don't need.

➢ Make it a habit to repeat this exercise at least once every three months.

Life in the Slow Lane

I lived on sailboat, where space was precious, for 15 years. The general rule was that you had to get rid of something whenever you brought in something new. The whole idea is to check and balance your life.

Now I'd like you to think about giving up activities that don't bring you pleasure. Don't overload yourself by saying yes to things that you really want to say no to. Don't volunteer for this and that, or take on too many jobs just to make ends meet. Don't schedule activities for every evening after work and then spend the weekends running errands. How can you get enjoyment from all this activity? And when do you have time to relax?

Then we pass on this frantic pace to our kids, expecting them to excel at everything. It's unrealistic and extremely stressful.

The Parent Trap

USA Today recently highlighted the plight of children whose parents overload their kids with too many activities. They push them to experience life to the fullest by scheduling activities every day of the week. From soccer to ballet to band camp, scout meetings, softball games, art classes and tutoring. It's just too much.

Kids need to be kids, and parents should let them do that. If you don't, you take a chance of your child experiencing burnout. They might feel they are living their parents' dreams and end up losing sight of who they are and what they want to do. The stress also affects mom and dad as they shuffle their kids from one activity to another.

Often parents become anxious when the child doesn't perform as well as other children. At Little League games I have witnessed dads becoming enraged when their child does not do as well as expected. The whole scene is loaded with anger, stress and fear; the child stands defenseless and shamed. Then those negative feelings come home and affect the marriage. Families can become dysfunctional and children might rebel, becoming withdrawn or acting out in unhealthy ways.

Rx #57: Lighten up. Live your life with integrity and let others live theirs; don't force anyone to comply with your rules, wishes or demands.

Tension experienced in childhood often gets embedded in psyche – and the amazing thing is that people rarely realize it. As an adult it can become hard to address those deep –seated issues.

Children can begin to feel stress as early as the age of five. Between six and twelve, stress becomes more pronounced, and at the onset of puberty it can escalate. Divorce is a major contributor to stress. New spouses, especially if they have children of their own, can magnify existing anxieties. Stress can affect teenagers very badly – and with the incidence of divorce so prevalent today many children must learn to cope with this anxiety producing situation.

Samantha was only four when her parents divorced. She went to live with her mother and rarely saw her father. Even now Samantha is overwhelmed by fear when her mother works later than usual. She panics (even though she is a college student) thinking that she will be left alone. On top of this, she still blames her mother for her insecurities, rather than accepting responsibility for herself.

This behavior, which is more common than you can imagine, is immature and counterproductive. Not only does it negatively affect Samantha's health, it maintains a wedge in the relationship.

That deep layer of anxiety which started early in her life continues. While she doesn't see this reaction as a problem, it keeps her adrenaline primed, ready to surge if her mother has not returned by a certain time. Although Samantha seems to live a normal life, her flight-or-fight induced stress level is in high gear. She came to see me complaining of nausea and headaches, two common signs of stress.

Over a series of months, we worked together so that Samantha could let go of this fear. She had to learn how to trust that her mother would be safe and that she would be too.

Rx #58: In order to let go of stress and anxiety rooted in your childhood, let go of your preoccupation of looking for someone to blame (usually a parent) and focus on love and forgiveness. Remember: Everyone really is doing the best that they can.

It takes time to uncover the forces that drive us. It requires patience and understanding to discover the ways we are tied to the past and why we project certain feelings into the future. I'm often asked about past lives and whether our previous life problems are carried into our present life. Whether you believe in past lives is not ultimately important; reducing your stress level is. Everyone has their own take on this subject. However, if you feel that information relating to a past life is valid, use it to your benefit.

But remember that even if you opt for long-term therapy, if you cling to self-righteousness you may not be able to solve your anxiety problems.

Get over it! I've had patients in their senior years still berating their long-gone parents for their problems. Most parents did the best they could at the time. Holding on to anger and bitterness to justify your own problems is self-indulgent and destructive. Stress drama cannot survive in an environment of love and forgiveness.

We must learn to peel away the layers of stress one at a time while appropriately reacting to thoughts, emotions and behaviors that arise. The key here is to be gentle with yourself and with your loved ones.

James was a very successful 30-year-old who earned a six-figure salary. Although he was considered a success by his parents and his peers, James felt his work was meaningless. He came to me confused about his purpose in life.

"What am I supposed to be doing?" He asked.

"The answer must come from within," I told him, "but I can help steer you in the right direction."

James learned several meditation techniques, and in the course of practicing them, came to the conclusion that his lucrative job was not satisfying his mission in life.

"I don't want to be seventy years old and feel I've missed out," he said.

James quit his job, and got a job with Outward Bound – an outdoor educational program – leading canoe trips in New York and Canada. Enthusiastic and filled with purpose, he became an inspirational and accomplished leader.

"Sometimes you just have to walk away from a job," he said, and I agreed. I once worked in advertising and knew about the daily corporate grind. Like James, I listened to my inner spirit and traded my ties for Hawaiian-print shirts. I not only survived, but I thrived.

"For me, a tie is a metaphor for shutting off the heart chakra," I told James when he returned from his first field adventure. "It's pulled tight against the throat like a noose. This closes off our ability to express thoughts and desires. This area is known as the speaking chakra, and is one of the seven energy centers in our body. Once the tie is tightened, it separates the head from the heart and you lose the ability to speak the truth."

Rx #59: Anything that constricts our throats also restricts our ability to communicate because it separates the head from the heart.

For me the corporate world is a contrived and manipulative workplace that lacks joy and a sense of fulfillment. I felt dishonest with my inner-spirit. Compromised by what I had been taught was the "responsible" thing to do, I finally surrendered to my poetic instincts and risked financial insecurity. Later I learned the true meaning of responsibility, which is "to respond to." That's what I did when I trusted my intuition and my deeper self. When I first dropped out of the corporate rat race, I received a lot of criticism from my family and friends. But, just like James, I found more happiness marching to the beat of my own drum.

Rx #60: When you find yourself being pulled in diverging directions, begin letting go of stress by paying attention to what you are doing. Be mindful of the things that create your tension. Figure out if there is a way to substitute a more pleasant, less stressful, activity. If not, choose to enjoy some aspect of what you are doing, even if you are not satisfied.

Past, Present & Future

Too often, we have a difficult time letting go of the past because we are attached to it. We may have regrets or guilt, about things we've done or things we have not done. It is almost impossible to move forward when you are worried about what will happen in the future.

Worry is not the same as being concerned. Being concerned is fine, because you are in touch with the situation and are making an

149

attempt to keep it under control. Worry, on the other hand, means you are not being proactive. Instead, you are buying into a negative state of mind.

Regret for decisions we have made can haunt us for years. Perhaps you took a job that didn't pan out, or got married with high hopes for a life together and it ended up in divorce court. Perhaps you broke up with a lover and now you want that person back. Maybe you decided not to have children and now, well past your child bearing, you want a baby. Or you made the opposite choice – you had kids and gave up a lucrative career.

Did you climb the corporate ladder and find it was all work and no fun, but now you're stuck because you're living beyond your means?

It doesn't matter. What does matter is that thinking your life could have been better keeps you rooted in regret, which keeps you stuck in the past. Accept that you have made these choices and decide to find ways to enjoy and appreciate them; this is taking responsibility for your happiness.

Another cause of regret is comparing your life to the lives of others around you. It's easy to feel unhappiness creeping in on you when your friends or family members have larger houses, more expensive cars or more money in the bank. Friends may seem like a perfect couple when you're alone or in an unhappy relationship, but don't be upset by what you perceive others have that you don't – that is a self-destructive illusion. You have everything you need to be happy right now. It is time to drop the "should haves" and concentrate on what we do have.

It's easy for me to tell you to let go. The truth is if I had to do it all over again, I would make some changes. Wouldn't we all? We learn from our experiences so that we don't keep making the same mistakes.

We do, however, need to accept our fallibility as human beings and, in the process, forgive ourselves and become happier people. Do not beat yourself up thinking that you made poor choices and that you'll be paying for them for the rest of your life. This will only keep you stuck where you are.

Accept this life is the one you have carved out for yourself – the good and the not so good parts. As long as you are alive, there is always time to make better choices and to create the life of your dreams.

Rx #61: There is always room to make new (and better) choices. However, it will mean letting go of the things that are holding you back from enjoying your time here on this planet.

Guilt and worry are two useless emotions that hold us back from fully savoring life. Guilt is usually the result of violating a rule, either yours or someone else's. It's unfinished business and it keeps you stuck in the past. Often the event that triggered that guilt happened so long ago you can't even remember what it was about. But if you can write about it or talk to a therapist, you may be able to find the root cause and move past it

It's even possible that you have bottled up guilt and regret and do not know it. When that happens, the thoughts and feelings can sap your energy, keep you up at night, or give you recurring headaches.

If any of the triggers below apply to your life, you can start working to unblock your chi and free yourself physically, spiritually and emotionally.

- I treated someone whose special to me poorly.
- I should have acted differently in a certain situation.
- I should have kept my mouth shut.
- I did something I wish I hadn't.
- I spend too much money.
- I start projects and don't complete them.
- I can't get motivated.
- I can't express my feelings.
- I have secrets I don't want to keep.
- I want to change.
- I don't like who I am.
- I can't love.
- I feel unlovable.
- I hate my body.
- I'm unhappy.
- I'm dissatisfied with my life.
- I want to stop _____ but I can't. (You fill in the blank.)

When you know where to look for the source of your guilt you can root it out of your body and your mind.

Rx #62: Once you discover the hidden sources of your dissatisfaction, you can start opening up your mind to release it, like butterflies leaving a net.

Developing Mindful Relationships

Pattie and Susan, divorced women in their early fifties, were best of friends. They went to dinner and out dancing; they walked and talked and enjoyed movies and plays together.

One of Susan's top priorities was sex. Her libido never abated and she was driven to find men to hook up with. Patti became Susan's sounding board and pseudo-therapist. At first, Patti found the sexual escapades amusing, but as the years passed, the never-ending drama grated on her nerves until finally, despite the fun they had together, she had to cut Susan out of her life.

"She was dragging me down, calling two and three times a day, with the same dilemma," Patti told me. "Susan kept making the same mistake, picking guys who only wanted to use her for sex, men who didn't want a committed relationship. She never seemed to learn and it bothered me that she didn't respect herself — so I lost respect for her."

Separating from a close friend, relative or colleague is a tremendous step in letting go. According to Eckhart Tolle, spiritual teacher and author of *The Power of Now* and *A New Earth,* when relationships (or other situations in life) hold you back or cause stress there are only three sane choices: accept it completely, change it, or leave it. Anything else causes unnecessary stress.

Rx #63: You are in charge. You are the master of your own well-being. All the options you need for optimal health are at your disposal. It is within your power to unlock the deep layers of stress and peel them away. You have the ability to reduce the daily worries that sap your strength and vitality. Until you realize this, you may not live up to your maximum potential.

Hannah, a 45-year-old secretary, ballooned to a whopping 350-pounds during an unhappy marriage. The floor shook when she walked and she was extremely conscious of her size. Her mother Betty berated her constantly about her plain face, large body and inability to keep a man.

When the doctor told Hannah that her health was in serious jeopardy, she opted for gastric bypass surgery. As the months passed, she shed pound after pound. Within two years, she was a size six, but her skin hung off her body.

"My mother finds fault with everything I do," Hannah said. "She says I'm ugly and that my body is disgusting, even though I've lost two hundred pounds. It's a steady stream of negative comments and I'm sick of it."

Despite the positive comments she received from her coworkers on her new shapely body, Hannah still needed her mother's approval.

"You have two choices," I said. "You can spend your entire life waiting for her to say something nice, or you can tell her to keep her negative comments to herself. Which do you want to do?"

Hannah said she would try to ignore her mother. But in the end, she couldn't shut her out. Instead, she stopped calling her, stopped going by for visits, and over the course of a year Hannah cut off all contact with Betty. "And look at this." She held out her hand and showed me an engagement ring.

"Congratulations," I said. "It looks like you've created a beautiful new life for yourself."

A year later I received a call from Hannah. Her self-esteem had continued to grow. Through her daily meditation practice she was able to accept her mother despite her faults. "Once I forgave my mother and accepted her unconditionally, her comments no longer bothered me," she remarked. "The funny thing is that she stopped criticizing me. Now we are the best of friends."

People will often discontinue unpleasant behaviors when we stop reacting to them and instead respond by taking care of our own needs.

Rx #64: It's up to you to set limits. If you allow others to push you around, you have no one to blame but yourself. Stand up for yourself. Stop playing the victim!

Most of the time we act more like robots than people. We walk around in a fog, hearing an endless litany of chatter in our minds. We don't listen to the birds or enjoy the sunrise or sunset. The years go by in a progression of nothingness that we call LIFE. We're on automatic pilot, never seizing the Golden Moments that will set us free. Caught up in mind games and emotional turmoil, the years pass us by without the happiness or joy we deserve. When you live on automatic pilot, you miss out on your own life.

There is good news however; life is constantly in a state of flux. That gives you a chance to go with the flow and learn from the ever-evolving changes in your midst. You still have time to find your true self and relish in your newfound happiness.

Rx #65: What happened in the past, or will occur in the future, is not important; what is important is the NOW.

The Golden Moment is upon you. When you are in tune with the present, you are being YOU. When you are in the moment, you are not trying to be someone you're not or live up to society's idea of who you should be. You are not the ideal employee, the perfect mate, the exemplary parent. You are YOU. Life can be pretty wonderful when you allow yourself to be your true self. The authentic self is happy and in harmony with the world around him or her.

Cara, a 39-year-old entrepreneur, opened a beauty salon on a shoestring budget. She didn't have much time to spare so she came to see me when she had a free day, which wasn't often.

"I have to move at a fast pace or everything will fall to pieces," she said. "If I stop to meditate I'll lose my momentum; I won't have the competitive edge that I need to survive out in the real world." The thought of doing a 30-minute body scan, which would have refreshed and renewed her spirit, frightened Cara. She was too busy (and scared) to stop.

"It will do you a world of good," I told her. But the tightness in her face made it clear that trying to convince her was like talking to a stone wall.

Now is the Time to Change

If you are living a life of high pressure, there is no end to the stress that will reside inside your being. Countless studies have proved that a calm mind and rested body will enhance your creative juices all day long. Unfortunately, many of us are caught up in a frantic frenetic world where the work ethic dictates endless hours of unadulterated stress.

There is no perfect stress reliever. Ashley likes the movies, Linda is ecstatic when she is skating. I enjoy tai chi, James is at peace when he is sailing. For some the stress-buster of choice is yoga, swimming, golf or Pilates.

Exercise provides countless opportunities for Golden Moments to be in "the zone." Being in the zone means that your body is alive and humming with the universe. It's an awesome feeling because you are totally in the NOW.

We live in a competitive and goal-oriented society, so guilt is often associated with the simple act of "nothingness," because it is considered a non-productive state. I remember how irritated I got whenever my dad said, "Son, you need to relax." If I had known how to relax, I would have. Most of us need to learn how to relax. Stress reduction is an art form that takes practice and persistence, the result of which is a more relaxed and joyful life.

Yet, we are "human beings," not "human doings." Being allows us to access the rich part of ourselves that inspires and regenerates our creative potential.

Rx #66: Every individual must create a method of winding down and relaxing. This quest must be done on a daily basis to maintain balance in this ever-challenging world.

The Golden Moment Meditation

Sit in a wooded area, perhaps on a river bank, and observe the divine action of Mother Nature. You'll see bees pollinating, ants at work, spiders building webs, tiny insects in motion, flowers swaying with the wind, pine straw, leaves and moss. Watch as though you are a participant.

This is your Golden Moment, your chance to go beyond your physical self. It's called "Letting Go." This Golden Moment of Meditation is really life's most pleasant and greatest lesson – forgiveness.

Before we can forgive others, we must first forgive ourselves. There are those little acts of selfishness, greed, jealousy, envy and other emotions that have permeated our lives at one point or another.

If you feel rejected, abused, ignored, or maligned in any way by someone else reciprocate with feelings of love. If you can't release the negative feelings, find a professional therapist or counselor who can help you. The opening of your heart is like extending your arms outward, palms turned facing the heavens. This gesture is one of receiving and shifts the energy from one of resentment or anger to one of peace and calm.

To forgive is to heal. Anger held inside creates disease. Forgiveness is the ultimate act of letting go. It puts us in a state of "ease" not "dis-ease."

Are you angry at someone? Do you feel hurt or rejected? Have you been criticized and want to get even? Guess what. You are human. This is a part of life we all face. While it may feel bad, you can change your reaction to what happens to you. But if you put up walls, whether in words or in silence, you become attached to that person or event – and that is not a good thing.

In other words, you are consuming what I call "emotional garbage." Just as you have a choice to eat nutritious food, you have a choice as to whether or not you absorb indigestible emotions.

How to Stop Digesting the Indigestible

Tai chi (which we discussed in the first chapter) is the source of all martial art forms. It is a moving meditation in which one wards off and neutralizes negative emotions and aggression that may come your way. The reason is scientific. If you do not oppose a force and instead move with it, you disarm its charge, causing it to lose energy.

The unkind words, accusations and guilt trips are not about YOU, so don't take them personally. Let the negative assaults come and go as if you were watching raindrops roll off your windshield. Here they come and there they go: Watch, observe, and don't cling to any of it.

Remember, it is about the other person, not YOU. If you really want to master the Art of Letting Go and living without fear, forgive yourself for letting it upset you and then forgive the other person. In your mind's eye (which is the place where we can access our power of vision when we close our eyes and focus), see yourself sending love to the person who hurt you. Actually think and feel this. And then extend love to the other person. Smile. Enjoy being a warrior of love and good intentions. Your life will always be full of joy and ease rather than stress and "dis-ease."

Rx #67: Becoming aware of the world inside yourself is a powerful way for you to let go of stressors in life. Forgiveness of oneself and others is payment in full. We then become Masters in the Art of Letting Go.

The Bearable Lightness of Being

Sometimes we put up emotional walls that block or sabotage our success. Like runners in a marathon, there is always a point where we think we can't go on. It's called "hitting the wall." Some people stop (a form of self-sabotage) by thinking they can't go on. But the truth is that they have the ability to keep going.

Others, determined to complete the challenge, tap into their inner strength to move through the barrier. What you learn on the other side is enlightening. Once you stare down the wall, you are able to physically and emotionally tap into a wealth of inner resources. This is called the runner's high.

Breaking through emotional walls is a daily commitment. It may seem as if you are not progressing when, in fact, you are. By being mindful with full intention and determination, you are traveling to a place of growth, comfort and evolution.

Once realized, you will see life differently. Maybe nothing has really changed. Yet a shift in perception can lead you out of the anxiety, depression and concern you once experienced. This will allow you to view yourself as a greater, more content and more fulfilled person. You will have broken through the wall and found success! This isn't just about racing, either. It can be in any area of your life: your career, your relationships, finances, weight loss, or achieving your present best.

Life is strange and wonderful. What seems like a wrong turn can be a blessing – a Golden Moment. When the world suddenly becomes crystal clear, the mental chatter will stop and you find serenity amidst any chaos. It is like a runner who's in the zone, even though he has hit the wall.

Rx #68: When you think about your life, can you see the upside to a downside situation? Can you enjoy the Golden Moments of your life?

Christa, a 44-year-old paralegal, was anxious all the time. Although she excelled at her job, her Type-A personality kept her on the edge. The lawyers she worked for always counted on her to perform with excellence and rewarded her diligence with pay raises.

One morning as she left for work, her car wouldn't start. Because she had a deposition at 8:30, she flew into a panic. Her heart began to pound and sweat moistened her upper lip. "I couldn't be late," she told me. "I HAD to be there on time."

Christa called a tow truck and then called work to say she'd be late. The attorney who answered sounded displeased, but the situation was beyond her control. Instead of panicking she began doing the eyelid relaxation exercise I had taught her, and within minutes she had transformed her thoughts. Instead of anxiety she was able to focus on the gorgeous day ahead of her. The sky was blue, it was dotted with exquisite clouds, birds chirped from the treetops and a gentle wind was blowing.

"Suddenly I realized that if I'm late, it's OK," she said. "The deposition will start without me. At that instance, I didn't care if it took all day for the tow truck to arrive. If my car had started, I would have missed this rare "Golden Moment."

Christa's revelation is a perfect example of being in the Golden Moment. Since there was no way to change the situation, she let go of the frantic desire to be at work on time and gave into the ebb and flow of life. Instead of being uptight and irritated, she found peace in her time of stress. There is a lesson here for all of us: Try to find something good the next time you're stuck in a traffic jam. Give up the notion of being on time – instead, be in the NOW.

Rx #69: When you are truly in the present you're in the Golden Moment. That's the perfect place to be. In the present there is no pain of the past or fear of the future.

Sadly, too many people miss out on these Golden Moments. They can occur at any time of the day or night, every day of the year, every year of your life. But for many people life is one big sprint to get to the future or relive the past. Many of these people have tunnel vision or no vision at all. And others simply don't get it. My friend Mark is one of those people. He still doesn't get it, although I've been talking with him for years about it.

Mark is a baby boomer, a 61-year-old retired corporate honcho who plays the stock market. Every morning before breakfast Mark logs onto the Internet to check the Dow Jones average. If it's up, he's happy. If it's down, even by a few points, his stomach churns. After a hasty cup of coffee and a bagel, he's back on the computer, e-mailing his broker to buy, sell or hold steady. He's always researching stocks, bonds and mutual funds. For him it's a full-time job.

"The market may or may not even out," I tell him. "And there's not much you can do about it. Go with the flow while doing your best."

"You don't get it, Edwin," he chides me. "This is VERY IMPORTANT; it's my life, my future and my retirement. What if I lose that?"

"Then you'll deal with it," I said. "Meanwhile you're missing today. Let's go for lunch and talk about it."

"I can't," he said. "I have to sell some stocks before they tank."

Mark is like the many men and women who are consumed by money and possessions that keep them rooted in the world of appearances. They think they have freedom of choice, but in reality they have no choice. They are stuck in a room with no way out and no key to the front door. The irony is that they have the key but they simply choose not to use it.

We have everything we need at this very moment. It's all right here. It's all perfect. You have the key to a perfect life. But if you keep the key in your pocket and fail to use it, you suffer the consequences.

Rx #70: It is fine to take a risk. In fact, it's often a good thing. But reality must play a part in this interface. You wouldn't jump out of an airplane without a parachute, so you must differentiate between logical intuition and irrational action. To make sure you know the difference you must listen to the voice within.

Our lives are often unpredictable. We don't know the outcome or the lesson in advance. That happened to me the first time I went to Mexico. It was there that I was offered a green energy drink. On my second visit I was curious about the contents of the drink. I was told that it was made from the Chaya plant.

For thousands of years it has been passed down by Mayans and Aztecs and used for both medicinal healing and nutrition, I was told.

I was told it is commonly referred to as "cura todo," which means "cure all." What was so interesting to me is that it had never been cultivated as a crop to sell or distribute. It was just grown and consumed in local households. The Maya considered Chaya not only a perfect food, but they used it as a primary herb for illnesses.

I heard how Chaya could cure diabetes, cleanse the blood, and regenerate liver function. Stories of its magical healing properties had become legendary. As I left Mexico I contemplated this information and began gathering more data. I also cultivated contacts in both Mexico and the Unites States.

Now, seven years later, Dr. Chaya nutritional products are on the verge of being seen in the marketplace. Today, a coalition of small commercial growers representing sustainable communities is growing Chaya. There are plans for an expanded product line including enzyme-rich raw energy bars, tea and energy drinks. Visit my website, www.stressreduction.com for more information on these products.

From the beginning, I had the connection to this miracle plant. Instead of letting my fears hold me back, I listened to that little voice and allowed my intuition to guide me. I was willing to risk all my personal assets while my peers were cautiously planning retirement. I let myself go and trusted my gut. Now, as the founder, I am actively pursuing business alliances and bringing Chaya-based products to the market.

Rx #71: The only thing holding you back from achieving your wildest dreams is you. Rewards are reaped when we trust our inner voice enough to take risks. The unknown can be the firecracker that sparks the fortune of tomorrow. Make sure you remember this.

If you learn how to let go of your fears, judgments, angst, worry and other destructive emotions, empowerment can be yours, because power resides in the one who is calm and who lives in the present moment.

It's important to remind yourself that you are a perfect being perceiving the world as imperfect. Knowing absolute truth on a conscious level is virtually impossible. Our mind (ego) gets in the way. It is our mind that sees imperfection. But we are not our minds; we are something much greater. Our essence – or divine nature – is the Truth of who we are. And this essence is perfect. It is the source of all life on this planet, and is a part of all of us at our core. We tap into this essence when we still our minds through regular meditative practices. The journey – for those who choose it – is to live close to this Holy Grail as spiritual warriors.

Being perfect does not infer that there is no room for growth. The external forms in our life, including our bodies, literally change with every breath we take. Our inner core and divine spirit, however, is always steady, unchanging and intact. So our experience here on Earth is one of learning how to move closer to home, to our true nature.

By releasing thoughts that put the emphasis on the outside world you are gaining power over your fears. Because, in reality it is quite the opposite – true power comes from within. If you want to prove it to yourself you can do a meditative exercise as a reminder that what seems threatening is, in fact, filled with wonder and simplicity.

Climbing the Mountain Meditation

Lie in a comfortable position, extending your legs, relaxing your arms at your side and gently closing your eyes. Imagine you're climbing a mountain and have provisions for a two-day ascent. As the climb becomes more difficult, you become increasingly aware of the weight of the heavy pack affecting your back and legs.

165

Determined to complete your mission and achieve a successful summit, you decide to unload items from your backpack. Open your pack now and choose what you need to leave behind in order to move onward. It may be a relationship, a job, or behaviors such as anger, ungratefulness or resentment and other negative emotions.

Consciously remove everything from the pack that has been holding you back in life. As you remove each item and place it on the ground, watch it shrivel into nothing. Once all the items have been removed, take a deep breath.

Now, imagine your new possibility is at the summit. See yourself in this possibility. Now zip up your pack and see yourself walking toward that summit. Feel the exhilaration of your lightened load and your new life.

What We See is What Sees Us

One day, as I got out of my car at the supermarket, I looked up and saw a magnificent double rainbow. It's sheer beauty and colors were so mesmerizing that I pointed it out to other shoppers. Most of them cast a brief glance upward, some thanked me, and others stared at me as if I had lost my marbles. After a short glance, most of them hurried to their cars. Not one person stopped long enough to admire the beauty of this rare occasion.

By letting go we recognize our interconnectedness with the world around (and within) us. But you must WAKE UP and PAY ATTENTION. Start today and let something go – a negative thought, a tiny piece of guilt, an article of clothing, a lock of hair, a person who's dragging you down – anything. A year from now you'll wonder why it took you so long to say goodbye!

Chapter 6

The Fear Factor

"To conquer fear is the beginning of wisdom." – Bertrand Russell

A quiz: HOW FEARFUL ARE YOU?

We can fear things like spiders and snakes and intangible ones like driving over a bridge, being alone after dark, not having enough money, or getting sick. Unknown fears are vague and often come out of nowhere.

Fear is the messenger that tells you to connect with your deeper self. It's that little voice described in the last chapter, your gut instinct. It may come as a dream or a flash while you are awake (an "aha" moment). It can manifest in many ways to capture your attention. Listen to this nagging and hear what it is trying to say to you. Or write it down in a journal so you can contemplate it later.

You know why? Because the answer is within you.

Here are a few statements and beliefs born out of fear. Have you ever said any of these out loud? Have you ever thought of them to yourself?

> ➤ I don't want to make out a will because that means I'm going to die.
> ➤ I don't want to die.
> ➤ I won't see a doctor; what if he finds something wrong?

- I'm constantly checking the internet to see if the pain I'm feeling can be fatal.
- I fear going to the hospital and being stuck with needles.
- I feel if I stop doing things, I'll shrivel up and die.
- Every time I go out in a car, I think I'll be in an accident.
- I check my tires constantly so I won't have a blowout.
- I never drive on the interstate because trucks make me nervous.
- I'm afraid of flying.
- I'm afraid of rejection so I never make the first move.
- What if my kids want to put me in a nursing home?
- I put off starting projects because I might not finish them.
- Why should I bother dieting? I'll always be fat.
- I can't sleep at night because I think I'll stop breathing.
- I'm afraid of being mugged or raped.
- I'm afraid my death will be painful.
- I'm afraid I won't have time to put my affairs in order if I die suddenly.

All of these statements originate from fear, and they keep the body primed for flight-or-fight. This stress syndrome eventually takes its toll, as I've said throughout this book. It's unhealthy. And now is the time to deal with it. See my website www.stressreduction.com for more suggestions on handling fear.

Fears that Produce Stress

There's a video that made its way around the world on the internet showing a group of people digging a hole in a wooded area in Europe. They lined the hole with plastic, filled it with water, and then covered it with leaves and twigs. With cameras poised, they waited for unsuspecting victims.

Two female joggers came along, talking and laughing and suddenly they're chest deep in water. The looks on their faces are shock and disgust. No doubt they're cold, because it is autumn. Next comes a single man jogging; he's in the pool as well. A bike rider is the next victim, tumbling head over handlebars. And so it goes.

The video is meant to be funny, but it's really a mean-spirited prank. It is however, an excellent example of how fear can easily be instilled. Do you think any of those unsuspecting victims will ever walk, jog or bike down a wooded path without an underlying anxiety that the ground will give way beneath them? I think not. That's the way stress compounds in our lives, one layer at a time.

If you've ever watched candle makers at work, you'll know that they take a white cord and dunk it in pots of hot, colored wax. After each dip, the candle is lowered into cold water to solidify it. Layers upon layers of heated wax are added, cooled and hardened. The analogy applies perfectly to stress. Humans are dipped in layers of stress, which harden over time around our core (the heart). When the candle is finished, a paring knife is used to peel back the colorful layers. As the design is created, different colors are exposed.

You must learn to pare away the outer layers of fear and anxiety until your essence is revealed. But the layers that surround your beautiful, gifted, authentic core are the fears that keep you from fully experiencing the joys of the universe. They might include:

Fear of being poor
Fear of accidents
Fear of illness
Fear of suspected illness

Fear of success
Fear of failure
Fear of rejection
Fear of being alone
Fear of aging
Fear of dying

Above all, it is the fear of the unknown that is the most harmful. The unknown can bring a lottery jackpot, a new lover, a most welcome surprise.

However, most of us dwell on the negative – a car accident, an illness, the loss of a job or a loved one, even death.

When we dwell obsessively about bad things, they often occur. Do we bring it upon ourselves? There are theories that say this is true, that what we focus on becomes our reality. But if we focus mostly on the positive – nature's wonders and the joyous events – they will come.

I'd be lying if I said that you only need to think good thoughts and nothing bad will ever happen. But if you can focus on the positive rather than the negative, the fear of the unknown will lose its grip on you because you'll be in the present (which is pure and positive). Even if something bad does happen, you'll be able to cope with it with steady balance and equanimity.

Rx #72: Focus on the positive, rather than the negative, and the fear of the unknown will lose its iron grip.

Andrew's Story – Enjoying Life

I met Andrew, a soft-spoken man originally from New England, walking along the beach. He was the former CEO of a cruise line and had taken early retirement at 48. After retirement he and his wife moved to Florida. As we walked and talked, he said: "I have everything one could desire. I'm financially secure, get along great with my kids, and I have a wonderful, adoring wife."

A few months passed and I would see them occasionally after my morning swim. Over time I noticed his former happy countenance was now haggard and drawn. I found this strange, since he used to grin from ear to ear. I caught up with Andrew one day when he was alone and we chatted. "How is it going?" I asked. "You seem stressed out."

"You have a keen eye," he said, managing a smile. Then he fell silent as we strolled down the beach.

After a few weeks Andrew confessed that he had so much time on his hands that he had become preoccupied with fear. He lost his joyful side and was consumed with negative thoughts all day.

"While I was working, I could handle dozens of phone calls every day, sometimes three or four at a time, and never feel overwhelmed, "he told me. "In fact, all those years when I was busy, my dream was to walk the beach without any responsibilities. Now I have everything I wanted and all I can think about is death."

Although dying is a major concern for some baby boomers, young people also have their own trigger points for stress. And they are no less real and just as important.

Ilene is a perfect example. The 32-year-old pregnant mother of two told me that "worry is my middle name" and said she frets about her in-laws because they constantly find fault with her homemaking and parenting skills.

"I worry about the kids constantly and drive myself nuts," she told me. "And of course I'm worried sick about this pregnancy; I wonder whether the baby will be healthy and how long it will take me to recover because I have two little ones at home."

Ilene was everywhere but in the moment. "Is the doctor concerned about your pregnancy?" I asked.

She shook her head. "He says I'm healthy as a horse. But my mind chatters away, constantly obsessing about awful things. I fret about unpaid bills, my kids getting into trouble, and how I'm going to handle the holidays. My husband, Greg, travels a lot for business, and when he's away all the responsibilities fall on my shoulders. Then when he asks me to come along for a relaxing weekend, I say no because I feel guilty about leaving the kids at home with a sitter. But then I also feel guilty about saying no to my husband. It's a no-win situation.

Rx #73: No-win situations are only in your mind. Life is a win-win as long as you take a breath and realize how glorious it is that you are alive. And that means that your possibilities are endless.

There is usually a cause for an underlying fear. For instance, if you fear an upcoming move across the country, go to a quiet place and think about your reason for this anxiety. You might miss your friends and family, or you might be worried about your new home. Once the fear is uncovered, it can be dealt with. When the fear is addressed, it will also have a less negative impact in your life.

Rx #74: Open your mind to the wisdom of your intuition. Allow yourself to face your fears and anxieties so you can address them and let them go. There is no time like the present to face your fears and deal with them.

Many of us buy into the idea that we are what we think. Since we often worry unnecessarily, we can get stuck in believing we are creating disease. But the body has an innate intelligence and knows better than to accept frightening thoughts. Right now there is an emphasis on New Age thinking that is inconsistent with the reality of your body's wisdom.

Just because a family member has died of cancer or Alzheimer's disease doesn't mean that it will happen to you. That's because there's only a three percent genetic predisposition to many health conditions. And yet some people jump the gun and do incredible things.

Look at your lifestyle. Your parents might be overweight, but you are your own person. If you eat moderately and exercise, then your chances of being overweight are slim. Their chosen path doesn't have to be yours.

Rx #75: You can design your own path to mental, emotional and spiritual wellness. You don't have to follow anyone else's lead.

The Chicken Little Effect

As individuals, we have a tendency to worry about a number of circumstances that may never occur – earthquakes, hurricanes, dust storms, drought, and asteroids falling out of the sky. I call it the Chicken Little Effect (you remember: "The sky is falling!") Fortunately for most of us, our innate wisdom knows better and does not buy into this fear-based thinking.

Living with fear means that you can't concentrate fully. Fear also means lost opportunities, poor performances and lost promotions. Fears and phobias will most likely cost you thousands of dollars over your lifetime. It will impact your health and restrict the quality of your life. It is not healthy to swim in the sea of negativity.

Let's examine the most common fears so you can see which ones apply to you. And let's look at a way to diffuse those fears.

Fear of being poor is a common anxiety that can usually be traced to messages we received as a child. Not having enough might have been a constant theme in your life.

Ellen came to see me about her financial anxiety. As a child her father often answered her request for money with the expression: "Do you think money grows on trees?"

If a dish or glass broke accidently, Ellen's mother became verbally abusive; she screamed that they were too expensive to replace. All hell would break loose if even the smallest thing was damaged. Ellen was so afraid of criticism that she once took pieces of a broken bowl and buried them in the back yard. Over time, money became a big fear for her – and for good reason.

As an adult, Ellen avoided all financial issues. Even her paychecks were automatically deposited into her checking account so she didn't have to deal with money. I pointed out to Ellen that she needed to change her relationship with money and see it as a reward for her hard work. Over time Ellen began to relax in the presence of money and appreciate her hard-earned wages.

Rx #76: Familiarize yourself with the language of money, which is a tangible source of energy.

Fear of accidents haunts many of us with a vague foreboding. Such fear is counterproductive and leads to expectation – and expectation is fear's breeding ground. It's an ugly circle of negativity. Your mental state can create the very situation that you are seeking to avoid.

Sam's fear of flash flooding in his low-lying area of Texas resonated through him like a sonic wave during a rain storm. Sam had a plan for evacuating his family and he was ready to put it into action at a moment's notice. When Sam heard reports of an impending storm, he packed everyone into the SUV and headed toward safety, despite assurances that his immediate area was not in danger. Midway to higher ground, Sam's vehicle was washed away by a flash flood, the very thing he feared the most. Luckily, Sam and his family were rescued. But when he returned home, his house had not been touched by water.

"I nearly killed us all because I was so afraid," he admitted. "I'll never do that again."

Rx #77: Irrational fear can interfere with normal functioning. This interference will upset your equilibrium and place you at a health risk.

The Fear Factor

Fear of illness in and of itself cannot bring on disease, but it can cause distress that over prolonged periods of time may result in disease.

Marie was diagnosed with cancer six years ago. She says she is not afraid of death; in fact, she told me she doesn't care if she survives her impending surgery.

"I'm sick and tired of the constant digging to get those rotten cells out," she told me. "But I'm really afraid of how deep they will have to go and what I'll look like when they're finished. That's what scares me."

Marie has cancer of the throat and tongue. She was diagnosed after years of drinking and smoking (a lethal combination). I taught her deep-breathing techniques to get her through the anxiety of her impending surgery and gave her a mantra to keep her anxiety at a minimum.

Despite that, she awakens at night drenched in sweat. It is the fear of her illness, combined with the fear of what's going to happen next that is really debilitating.

Rx #78: Always assume you are in good health and focus on the positive functioning of your body. If you have a specific health problem that needs medical attention, see a medical professional.

Fear of suspected illness: There is a term for persistent, abnormal, and unwarranted fear of becoming ill. It is called Nosophobia, which is derived from the Greek "nosos" or disease. Webster's Dictionary defines it as a "morbid dread of disease."

Symptoms typically include shortness of breath, rapid breathing, irregular heartbeat, sweating, nausea and a feeling of dread. Everyone experiences a fear of illness at times, but if it is prolonged and intense, the unconscious mind will begin to think: This could be happening to me.

Or you may feel or imagine you have the symptoms of the illness and therefore create the illness within your being. Remember, you create your own reality, so make it a healthy and serene one, not the picture of illness.

Folk singer Woodie Guthrie left a legacy of songs that are still popular today. He died in 1967 from Huntington's Chorea, a hereditary degenerative disease of the nerves. Woody's mother died of this same debilitating disease. The question remains: Did she pass it on to her son Woody? And did Woody pass it on to his son, another popular folk singer, Arlo Guthrie?

By the time Arlo was a young man, science had devised a test to determine whether he had the genetic disposition for inheriting the family disease. When offered the test, Arlo declined saying: "If I'm going to get it, I don't want to know. I don't want that worry hanging over me for the rest of my life."

While you might not develop a disease from your family genetic pool, your subconscious mind can inherit troubling thought patterns. The end result of troubling thought patterns, including fears, is a compromised immune system, which leaves the door open for illness. The index of resistance varies for each person. When someone is robust, the threshold is high. Those with a delicate or weak physical condition have a low threshold. The thing to be most aware of is that dwelling on illness may or may not cause you to develop a disease, so why take the chance? Wouldn't it be better to invest your thought power in creating and maintaining a new exercise or eating program, both of which are helpful in strengthening the immune system?

Like all fears and phobias, the fear of illness is created by the unconscious mind as a protective mechanism. Many of us have experienced events in our past that linked illness or emotional trauma to our being. While the original event may have been a real situation, the condition could possibly be triggered now by seeing a movie, a medical TV show, or someone you care about getting very sick.

There are drugs that treat phobias of illness, but the side effects and withdrawal symptoms are often quite distressing. Also, drugs can only temporarily suppress your symptoms; the only true way to root out phobias and fears is through meditation and breathing techniques, hypnotherapy, or counseling that gets to the cause of the distress. You can't solve a problem unless you know the origin of it – and only then can you eliminate it. Visit my website www.stressreduction.com for a list of recommended books on the subject of health and healing.

Rx #79: Living in fear that you will become ill is one sure way of missing out on the beauty of your life right now. The now is all we have at this moment. So why waste it worrying about the maybe.

The mind is so powerful that it can render you a hypochondriac. This intense fear of being ill can actually cause physical manifestations of the real diseases. Common symptoms include headaches; abdominal, back, joint, rectal, or urinary pain; nausea, itching, diarrhea, dizziness or balance problems. Many hypochondriacs feel they are not understood by doctors and become frustrated by a lack of relief. (Note: some diseases are not understood by doctors although they are real. When someone tells you it's all in your head, make sure you have exhausted all possibilities and done your research.)

In the past, phobias manifesting as hypochondria were considered untreatable. However, scientific studies have shown that cognitive behavioral therapy is an effective treatment option.

Therapy, tension-releasing tai chi and chi kung can also help a hypochondriac cope with the physical symptoms and emotional worry. This, in turn, helps reduce the intensity and frequency of troubling bodily symptoms.

Fear of success sounds like an oxymoron, doesn't it? Who wouldn't want to be successful? You may have a short-term or long-term goal, but you just can't seem to take the steps you need to make it happen. So, what's holding you back?

It's called fear of success, and it is a common malady. Fear of success is often derived from a sense that you don't believe that you are worth much (commonly called low self-esteem). When we don't feel worthy, we don't feel that we deserve good things, including money. It can be an insidious challenger, more powerful than fear of failure because fear of success is almost always unconscious. The problem is not a fear of success in itself, but rather the fear of what success will bring.

Marianne came to see me with this very problem. She was 51-years-old and had worked as a waitress for most of her adult life. Marianne wanted to open her own café, and even though she had found the perfect storefront she was too paralyzed to move toward her goal.

"What's the problem?" I asked during our first session.

"I can't put the pieces of the puzzle together," she said. "I have the space and the money set aside, so that's not an issue. I find myself in a state of inertia."

"Are you afraid the café won't be successful?" I asked.

"On the contrary," she said. "I just can't get into the flow to move forward."

"Fears that are not evaluated consciously have a tendency to grow stronger," I explained. "When you avoid something you fear, either consciously or subconsciously, you automatically reinforce the behavior. So when you avoid working on your goal because of a hidden fear of success you actually reinforce the act of not doing. As time passes, it becomes harder and harder to get yourself to take action."

I sent Marianne home to think about this. The next time she came to see me, I asked her: "What will happen if you do manage to achieve your goal and open the café?"

She thought a long time about it and said: "I don't think I'll have a life. I won't have any free time to relax and unwind. I'll never be able to take a vacation, and my passion is traveling."

It's not a bad thing when fears surface. In Marianne's case her fear indicated that there was something more to discover. She listened to her inner guidance, and eventually found out what was at the core of her hesitation. Because she took the time to understand her fears and desires, Marianne was able to make a better decision.

Trudy's Story – Weighting for Others

Trudy came to me with a similar problem; however, her goal was to lose 145 pounds. When I asked Trudy what the problem was, she told me she didn't want people looking at her.

"They look at you now," I told her.

"Yes, but now they accept me as the fat girl in the office, and I'm used to that. If I lose weight, then I will lose my eating buddies. They're my best friends and they are quite overweight. We go to the movies together and then we all have dinner together. They won't want me around if I'm thin because I'll make them feel bad about being so large."

"So it's a social issue?" I asked.

"Yes," she said. "And what if I buy all new clothes and then put the weight back on? People will think I'm a real loser."

Success isn't always a bed of roses. Change can elicit both positive and negative feelings. Some people claim they want to succeed, but the reality is that their negative conditioning outweighs their positive thoughts about it and their fears are so strong, they cancel out the positive outcome.

One way to overcome this problem is to sit with the fear that is holding you back from reaching your goal. Look inside the body and notice where the fear is; "watch" it and you will see it begin to dissipate. Dig up the negatives, and look closely at them asking "Is it really true?" You will often find that these fears are not rational; nor do they serve your current life stage. Uprooting a negative thought may eliminate it completely. The alternative is to learn coping skills for going beyond your fears rather than being paralyzed by them. This is often called "feeling the fear and doing it anyway."

Remember the two-minute breath exercise? This is an example of a skill that can be applied to overcome fears. Breathing consciously forces us to slow down. It creates space and allows us to separate from fearful thoughts and the anxiety they produce.

Take a deep breath then release it as slowly as you can. Bring awareness to the place in your body where you feel the fear or anxiety. Now take another one or two slow, deep breaths, while paying attention to this area of the body. Notice what is happening.

With this simple breathing technique we can consciously release our fears as they arise, before they wound or immobilize us. Through breathing we can quickly regain our balance (homeostasis) and restore peace and confidence.

This book provides many exercises like this to assist you in releasing stress and restoring balance to body, mind and spirit. Refer to the index in the front of this book or visit my website, www.stressreduction.com and select what works best for you in the moment. If one exercise does not do the job, then pick another. At times when we are very anxious or jittery, it may be best to first take a brisk walk or do some form of physical exercise (consider chi kung). Releasing excess energy prior to attempting meditation or breath work is always helpful.

When practiced regularly, these exercises bring us – with increasing frequency – into the present moment. In the present moment we are calm and clear, and capable of making sound decisions. We act from our essence rather than our ego. It is the only solution for successfully and peacefully resolving the inevitable trials and tribulations of human existence.

Rx #80: It is always helpful to focus on the positive side of your goals.

You know why – because fear has a tendency to shrink under direct scrutiny, making it easier for you to go beyond it. That, in turn, allows your subconscious conditioning to weaken its hold on you.

For example, if you lose weight, you'll need new clothes. If that puts a strain on your budget, you might sabotage your efforts to lose weight. Once you examine the situation and figure out a way to deal with it, you can then send a message to your subconscious that you needn't fear this problem because you have it solved.

Suppose you ask yourself, "What will happen if I succeed?" And you find the answer is that the negatives outweigh the positives. In this case, chances are you'll find that the goal you've set for yourself is not in sync with your heart center. And that is where your emotional barometer is. Your heart will never steer you wrong; it will tell you what is good for you and what will conflict with your highest good.

In the long run, Marianne decided not to open the café. Once she heard herself say the words "traveling is my passion," she decided that being stuck in a café day after day was not what she wanted. Within six months she had become a tour guide.

Chet came to me for a few counseling sessions when he hit a roadblock in writing country songs. Chet was a 47-year-old father of three who lived in Texas.

"My songs could be hits," he told me. "I think I have the talent to make it."

"Sounds like you're ready to go for it," I said. "What's the problem?"

Chet stroked his beard, and I could almost hear him churning over thoughts in his brain. "Everyone says I have to move to Nashville," he said. "I can't see uprooting the whole family just so I can live my dream."

"Why not?" I asked. "People do it every day."

"It doesn't seem right."

"It takes courage to create," I told him, "Creativity is often followed by guilt because you've changed the order of the status quo. You stepped out of your comfort zone and you wonder if you've done the right thing. You wonder will it pay off or will your family suffer. Does that make sense?" I asked him.

Chet nodded. "Yes, it does. I think I'm not ready to upset the apple cart right now – maybe in the future, when my kids are grown."

The result was that Chet put his dreams on hold, but he continued to write songs in the hope of someday he'd have a hit.

The weight attached to being successful can be frightening. It's a creative dynamic that may lead others to believe you are smarter, richer and more powerful than they are. If you're not comfortable with these labels you might thwart your own success. Or you might be afraid that you will fail and people will think you're not very smart.

Rx #81: Success is a creative entity that can upset the apple cart. It may create a sense of guilt and feelings that you don't deserve it. That's why healthy self-esteem is a good thing to have before you chase your dreams. The reason is that you have to step out of your comfort zone and face any doubts that prevent you from achieving happiness and success.

The Fear of Rejection

Fear of rejection can cause one to feel uncomfortable in groups and avoid meeting new people. Whenever there is a possibility for rejection, some people feel afraid. Fear of rejection is increased by the value you place on the others in your life.

Some people suffer more intense fears of rejection than others. Deeper issues may be at work here, such as childhood abandonment issues stemming from divorce, fear of being alone, or fear of not being able to take care of oneself.

The thought of being alone is not, in itself, something to fear. If you believe that you can take care of your own needs, then being on your own can be liberating. However, if you believe that you need someone else to take care of you or to make you happy, then you will become dependent on others to fulfill your emotional needs, and that is a recipe for disaster.

Rx #82: Examine the degree to which you can create your own joyful experiences. Be aware that too much dependence on others can undermine your confidence in yourself, and cause a greater fear of rejection.

If your self-image is based on what others think of you or how well you are liked, then fear of rejection can be a threat to your whole being. If being well-liked, married, a good mom or a caring dad, an entrepreneur or an artist is the way you want others to see you, then anything that threatens those things can lead to stress. But this is the human condition, so don't get too carried away beating yourself up. Everyone wants to be liked in some ways.

Remember Russ, whose in-laws couldn't accept the fact that he wanted to be an artist (a reaction which caused him migraines?) That was the direct result of wanting his in-laws to accept his creativity. They were people he held in high regard and he wanted to please them, but couldn't.

Rx #83: To overcome the fear of rejection you must define yourself in a way that doesn't make you dependent on what others think of you.

But that is much easier said than done. It all starts with an appreciation of yourself – of who you are and what you are. We all have wonderful qualities and a few not-so-great behaviors. But when you accept yourself and stop worrying about the opinions of others, your happiness will increase tenfold.

The Fear of Being Alone – The Human Condition

The fear of being alone is an issue that affects most of us. While there are many people who derive great satisfaction from living alone or with a pet, the majority of us want someone to share our lives with. There is nothing wrong with this. But it becomes wrong when you choose someone who makes your life miserable and does not validate you.

Fear of rejection, fear of unfaithfulness and fear of loss when you are with someone creates a high level of anxiety that can increase when coupled with a fear of being alone. The more emotionally attached you become to someone – and the more important you think they are to your survival – the more anxiety you might have about losing them and the less likely you are to leave them, no matter how unpleasant the relationship. Remember, the anxiety you feel is created by YOU; nobody else has done this to you. It is our thoughts and perceptions about other people's behavior and the resulting fears that produce the anxiety.

It's easy for me to tell you to control your fears of rejection by not becoming overly attached to people. But that would be oversimplifying a critical juncture in healthy development. This is a very important issue and one that's not easy to conquer – but it can be done. Meditation, therapy, counseling, hobbies, successful ventures and a support system can keep these feelings at bay.

Rx #84: The greater your attachment to a significant other, the greater your fear of rejection might be.

Matt and Donna came to me for marriage counseling. They met at a business function and fell head over heels in love. While they seemed like a happy couple, Matt confessed that he gets upset when Donna goes on a business trip, and Donna admitted that she isn't happy when Matt goes to sports bars with friends. The situation was driving a wedge between them and they needed help.

"You have to understand that the more you cling to each other the more anxious you will be," I said. "Many people develop a fantasy about what love should be like. But fantasizing about the future has the ability to cause anxiety over unmet expectations."

I added that Donna's business trips and Matt's sports bar adventures were putting them both on an emotional roller coaster.

"You will drive each other away by being too emotionally needy if you continue this behavior." I told them

They decided to become more trusting of each other when they were separated. Donna told Matt that her business trips were strictly business and he had nothing to worry about. Matt told Donna that he would cut down on his frequency at sports bars and admitted that he found her more fun to be with anyway.

Rx #85: To prevent an emotional roller coaster ride with your partner, don't plan the future prematurely. Always know that the relationship may not work out, so be sure to have a hobby, activities and friends outside the relationship that bring you joy.

To Age or Not to Age – This is the Question

The fear of aging is something that we all fall prey to at some time in our lives. The aging process begins the minute we reach our late thirties and forties. Both men and women see their skin lose elasticity and signs of aging become more pronounced.

That's the nature of getting older. Everyone faces it at some point in time. There are ways to avoid this malady – plastic surgery, laser treatments and facial creams are effective ways to maintain a youthful appearance.

Some men experience erectile dysfunction later in life, especially if they have diabetes or prostate problems. Luckily, there are little blue pills to put the zip back into your sex life. Both men and women, however, will see signs of aging they wish would stop. Don't worry; it's just gravity doing its thing.

The most common phrase heard around the swimming pool at senior communities is "I never thought it would happen to me." But unfortunately, the surprise is on us all. And it's not as bad as it seems, especially since we know that with age comes wisdom.

Surrender to What is Happening Now

Dwelling on things you have no control over raises anxiety levels. If you want to lower your stress, you must embrace the aging process head-on. It's easy for me to tell you not to worry, but I can tell you from experience that we must work with what we have. Fear will do nothing to change things or make them better. But doing something with your life does. If you look at age as a time to make changes in your life, then you are using your gifts wisely.

The goal is to realize that aging is not such a bad thing. So stop obsessing about it. No matter what age you are, it's important to keep a healthy attitude and stay physically active. People who played a lot of tennis in their youth often take up walking or golf, which is less strenuous. Yoga, tai chi and swimming are wonderful exercises for anyone, no matter what your age.

Rx #86: Remember, you are as old as you feel. It's best to live your life making the most of your physical and mental abilities. If you feel old you will be old. If you feel young, you will be young (age is just a number, remember?)

Age is Just a Number

Fear of dying is the most overwhelming fear. Baby boomers, who always felt exempt from their final curtain call, are now facing their own mortality. Some people don't like the prospect of death, while others are not afraid of this mystical journey.

For the most part, fearing death is a waste of time. Whether you choose to ignore it or become morbidly obsessed by it, there's nothing you can do except enjoy the NOW. It is truly all we have.

Although death is not something to obsess about, it is a motivating factor to put your affairs in order. That means appointing an executor for your estate, getting a health care power of attorney, creating a living will and making funeral arrangements. In other words, protect and provide for your loved ones. You'll feel a sense of peace and relief once those things are in order. Some people stare death in the face by living on the edge. They live life to the fullest, bungee jumping, racing cars, climbing mountains, and going shark hunting.

Mark Rackley is one of them.

Rackley began a career as a spear fisherman in the Florida Keys at the age of 18. He filmed sharks and got footage while riding hammerhead sharks. He would hold the camera with one hand and hold onto the shark's fin with the other!

Rackley now consults with marine biologists in shark infested waters and relies on his gut instincts to stay safe. The only real occupational hazard is the "close call," where anything can happen. Once, in the Everglades, a 12-foot alligator slammed into his camera and almost took a bite out of him.

But what about the fear factor? Rackley admitted that if he obsesses about death he would never be able to get into the water. "Steve Irwin's death gives you a little taste of reality," he said when talking about the late crocodile hunter from Australia who died from a sting-ray barb to the heart. "The things we do are very dangerous. People warn us that it's going to end in tragedy, but we always come out alive. In my heart, I don't feel like I'm ever going to die."

Frankly, Mark will die, hopefully in a peaceful way and not face-to-face with a shark or gator. I subscribe to the philosophy of Star Trek's Spock: "Live long and prosper."

Rx #87: To challenge your fears about living and dying, try to change the order and pattern of your daily existence. Take a different route to work, shop at a different grocery store, or eat on a different schedule. Be spontaneous – get out of your rut.

It's not important what you choose, but it is important to know you have options and adventures to experience. Plan and do those things that you most want. If you do this, when the time comes to face death it won't seem so awful – you will have lived your life to the fullest.

Phobias and fears can be so all consuming that they immobilize and drain you of all joy. Here is a helpful acronym for F.E.A.R.: False Expectations Appearing Real. The key word is "appearing". Most of what we imagine in our mind that causes fear is false and will likely never happen. So let go of it and focus on what is in front of you in the present moment.

While it's always good to plan for the future, being in the NOW is the best way to avoid anxiety. After all, if you're breathing then you're obviously not dead – and that's a good thing.

Rational planning is not the same as obsessing. Eating a reasonable diet and getting enough exercise will help you live a full life. Cultivate hobbies you love; that will add to your happiness. Beyond that, you have to work on letting go. In order to let go you'll have to understand that it makes no sense to worry about things you cannot control.

Rx #88: Training the mind to focus on things you have control over – and letting go of things that are impossible to change – are the best antidotes to anxiety and phobias.

Journaling is an excellent way of getting in touch with your feelings. Write down what is bothering you and what makes you happy; this is not a journal for someone else to read. The goal is to silence the internal censor that blocks your ability to live life to the fullest. The best time to do this is when you're experiencing anxiety.

My client Molly always kept a journal. I asked how it affected the quality of her life.

"I feel as if the pleasant experiences become more evident and I am able to let go of the challenging things in my life," she said. "Now I look forward to journaling about the things I love about my life."

Keeping a gratitude journal emphasizes the positive things in your life. It also releases the negative patterns that victimize you.

Andrew felt lousy after he retired. He confessed to me that he felt like a victim of his own internal chatter and fear of death. His workaholic behavior had been a distraction to him for years. Now that he had so much time on his hands Andrew began obsessing about aging. I suggested that he write about his fears about aging and the suffering, dependence, separation and loss of control that he was imagining.

"Do you ever swim in the ocean?" I asked.

"No," he said.

I explained that the ocean is a healing pond. Aside from the presence of negative ions that remove toxins and balance the body, the sea is a resource to alleviate anxiety and promote healing. Since our bodies are 75 percent saline solution (or water) swimming in the ocean is like returning to the womb.

"We are the ocean and the ocean is within us," I said. "Surrendering to the power of the ocean and its vastness frightens a lot of people. But swimming in the ocean on a daily basis is a symbolic gesture of confronting our own mortality."

As a leader, Andrew was accustomed to making decisions and taking risks, so I was happy to hear that Andrew was swimming in the ocean and facing his fears. He enrolled in a six-week hospice training course working with people facing death. At the end of his training, Andrew felt that he better understood this final act in life. He also felt more comfortable about the process of aging.

Rx #89: Fear makes people feel isolated and alone, yet it is part of the growth process. When we feel alone we become more compassionate with ourselves and others. In facing our fears, we become fearless warriors.

Managing Fear-Based Stress

By definition we are one-of-a-kind individuals. That is our birthright, our sacred gift. What we do with our lives depends on the choices we make – no one has the right to judge us. A street bum may be much happier than a corporate CEO, and yet society frowns on the lifestyle of the down and out.

Only you can determine what the true definition of success is. If your life is filled with anxiety, stress and unhappiness, look at your fears and see how you can become more accepting or find the courage to go out and get what you want.

Poverty Consciousness – Not a Great Place to Reside

Remember Ellen's story? She was unable to let go of the shame, frustration and anger surrounding her money issues. Money took precedence over her emotional well-being and she made "money love" her priority. She had a deep conviction that her parents valued money more than they valued her. For Ellen "money is the root of all evil" took on an entirely different meaning.

Over the years, Ellen learned many things that could have helped her, but she was unable to follow through until she was almost bankrupt. This brought her to my office. Creative visualization exercises helped her see a more positive side to money that ended up reducing her anxiety and preventing her from needing to file bankruptcy. Together we programmed positive messages about money that had a healthier tone.

Exercises like tai chi and chi kung (see my website www.stressreduction.com for instructional DVD) are helpful for clearing blockages and stagnation in our bodies. The energy flow or "chi" is restored to proper balance. In a similar manner, visualization can be incredibly useful for removing mental blocks around money and other matters. Negative judgments about it, or fixed ideas on how or when it can come, block the possibility of receiving it in abundance.

I explained to Ellen that money is not the root of all evil. It's the love of money – and the valuing it above all else – that can create problems. Money, like everything else, is simply a form of energy. Typically we exchange this form of energy for another, for example trading money for work or money for a computer.

We give money its meaning; it can be an ally or an enemy. We can push it away by saying things like "money isn't important to me," or we can receive it with grace and thankfulness and allow it to flow in.

Once Ellen altered her perception of money as the root of all evil and visualized what her life would look like – and how she would feel – with unlimited wealth, the money flowed in. Essentially, she shifted from "poverty consciousness" to "prosperity consciousness."

Rx #90: Don't be intimidated by money. If you need help managing money or balancing your checkbook, ask for it. Become conscious when you are handling money and you will become more comfortable with your finances. Forget get-rich-quick schemes, however. They are usually just that – schemes.

Fear of Accidents

The best thing when confronting your fear of accidents is to become optimistic. Whenever you feel anxious that an accident is coming about, push it away. This won't prevent it, but your positive thoughts will stop the mental pictures that float through your mind. Imagine yourself arriving at your destination in good spirits. Look to the goal, rather than the journey.

Rx #91: Make it a habit to fill your mind with thoughts of happiness and safety.

Drinking From the Well of Health and Wellness

Picture yourself in good health, even though you may have some issues to address. Regardless of what seems wrong, think of all the things in your life that are right. In other words, stop dwelling on the negative. You know why? Because what you think about you bring about.

That doesn't mean that you should ignore your health problems, it just means you can be proactive in resolving them without becoming obsessive. Obsessing about the negative things in your life can make you feel hopeless, and that can sabotage your good intentions.

Give yourself a mantra that harmonizes with your daily life and with the universe. Cultivate a mind that is confident and wants to live to a ripe old age, hearty and happy.

Take charge of your health by staying as fit as possible, but if you know something is out of the ordinary be proactive and seek medical advice. If that medical advice is not satisfactory, continue to seek help until all your questions have been answered.

Don't allow yourself to be intimidated by professionals just because they have a lot of medical degrees. You must be your own health advocate. There are wonderful resources for getting and staying healthy: visit my website www.stressreduction.com for more information.

Fear of Illness

If you are worried about having a serious medical problem, despite receiving reassurance to the contrary, keep a journal. Describe the symptoms, episodes of illness, dates, times and what might have set them off. It will allow the physician to see a closer link between the symptoms and external events.

Maintaining a healthy lifestyle, which includes eight hours of sleep, eating well-balanced meals, socializing and having a positive outlook, can increase your chances of staying healthy. Practicing relaxation techniques, such as breathing, meditation, tai chi, chi kung or yoga will help decrease anxiety and stress.

Replace worries with activities that will fully engage your mind or body and allow you to shift gears. You can try games, hobbies, exercise, movies, talking with a friend, or strolling through a museum.

Rx #92: Break your worry habits one step at a time.

Fear of Success

If you are pursuing a career to please others (living out your parents' dream), instead of following your own instincts, you will miss out on the path to success. On the other hand, taking a detour may lead to your ultimate happiness. Just look at Marianne, who made a U-turn midstream and found that instead of owning a café she really wanted to travel. She would have been unhappy stuck in the same place day after day.

Again, all I can say is that you should listen carefully to that little voice within, which is your gut. It will tell you what is best for you despite anyone else's advice.

Rx #93: Success comes from within, not from outside. Taking risks in life and following your intuition are mandatory to evolve and discover happiness. Know the difference between intuitive action and irrational behavior. The wrong choice usually comes from running away from the self.

Fear of Rejection

If you define yourself primarily as someone who must be loved and accepted by others, then your happiness will be in THEIR hands, not yours. Start by making a list of eight characteristics that describe you.

Now, is there anything you'd like to change or add? If not, then learn to accept yourself. Once you like who you are, it becomes less important who likes or loves you. When you like yourself and feel self-confident, people will be drawn to you. Likewise, if you hate yourself, why would you expect anyone else to like you?

If you believe there is only one solution for you and your life isn't worth living without this person, you are adding unnecessary fear. The truth is that there are many people who could be the perfect partner for you. Keep your mind and heart open to new possibilities.

Rx #94: The less confident you are about being able to create a happy relationship, the more likely you will pick someone who will not treat you well.

Don't just go along for the ride when you see red flags waving (remember to listen to that little voice). And beware of a needy partner who can have a negative, draining effect on your happiness. They are called energy vampires and can be quite debilitating.

Fear of Being Alone

Studies have shown that lonely people create damaging stress hormones in their bodies. Over time, the toxic stress may lead to sleep disorders and other health problems caused by an elevated epinephrine level. This hormone increases heart rate and elevates blood pressure. The symptoms and results are basically the flight-or-fight response, which means stress reactions are in overdrive.

Lonely people tend to feel threatened by difficult situations; however, sharing life events increases pleasure and reduces stress. Being with someone you care about builds closeness and intimacy. That's why it's important to maintain contact with friends and family, even if you have had differences over the years.

Sharing important life events and feelings helps build solid relationships that become a power source for attachments. This can be positive if both partners come into the situation as equals, but negative if one person is pulling away or is involved in destructive habits.

Yelling, physical violence, verbal abuse, constant neediness, alcoholism or drug dependence do not contribute to a viable and loving relationship. Ask yourself: Am I better off with or without this person? The answer is simple: You're better off alone than with someone who drags you down or makes you feel bad about yourself.

Rx #95: Maintaining close ties to family and friends reduces the fear of being alone. Even if you don't have a significant other, surround yourself with people you like, or join social activities to promote good mental and physical health.

One of the ways to avoid being lonely is to socialize. Find a club that interests you, ask a neighbor over for lunch, volunteer in a church or some other setting that will bring you joy. If you still work, find a colleague to buddy up with for dinner or attend a movie after work or on weekends.

If you are socially active but still feel alone, try establishing a closer bond with someone. Adopt a pet and you'll never be alone. Above all, get off the pity pot and stop feeling sorry for yourself. DO something about it!

Fear of Aging

We live in a youth-obsessed culture. Movie stars are considered over the hill when they pass forty. As we age, many of us feel lonely or unlovable – a feeling that intensifies with each passing birthday. We feel the best kept days have passed us by and that the future is bleak.

That's pure hogwash! Your later years can be filled with joy, promise and the exquisite fulfillment of dreams. Financially secure and unencumbered by children, the silver and golden years hold the promise of making every dream come true. People meet and marry well into their nineties, and the dreams you fantasized about can become realities.

Here are a few ways to manage your stress about aging:

➤ *Cultivate friends.* Stay in contact with family members and make new friends with neighbors or people you meet at social events. Take up a new hobby that taps into your soul and fulfills you.

➤ *Connect with your spirituality.* Find a place of worship where you'll feel comfortable. Here you will meet new people and get to socialize. Try meditation groups, prayer groups, or find a spiritual connection that suits your personality on a deep level. Many people at these events are open to new friendships and soul bonds.

➤ *Volunteer.* Volunteering is a great way to open the heart and fulfill your inner self. Animals, older adults and children of the planet need your help. Tap into your inner charity zone and give back – if not with money, then with time and energy.

➤ *Exercise your intellect.* Reading, taking classes at a local college, playing Scrabble or other games, doing crossword puzzles, going to the movies, or joining discussion groups.

➤ *Nurture your creativity.* Find a hobby or other outlet for your artistic impulses. Try new recipes, gardening, take up writing, drawing, painting, scrap-booking, or acting – anything to keep your body and mind filled up with positive hormones. Try something you've never done before.

➤ *Enjoy nature.* Whether you walk on the beach, hike in the woods, relax in the mountains or sail the seas, try breathing deeply – it will give you a sense of being grounded in the Universe. Being one with nature provides Golden Moments.

Rx #96: Try to set aside your fears and anxieties and welcome the journey ahead. Embrace the gift of aging with a positive attitude.

Fear of Death

You can wear a seatbelt when you drive and a life jacket when you sail, but eventually you'll face the moment of truth. For some it will come too soon. For others it will be past due and a welcome relief from bodily pain and suffering.

Sidney and Caroline, a devoted couple who'd been married for 33 years, came to my office in deep fear and grief. Sidney's doctor had told him that he had only a few weeks to live and they were despondent. As avid travelers, they'd planned a five-year itinerary for their future. The three of us sat in my office as they flipped through their photo albums. As they began to take stock of their warm memories, the grief shifted to joy. Sidney and Caroline realized their lives together had been a celebration of love. The happy faces of their children and grandchildren were a testament to the strong family bond they shared.

Some of Sidney's fear began to subside as he experienced a deeper connection to family. Once he was in a more accepting frame of mind, Sidney planned to record messages and stories on tape for family members. They reconnected with a spiritual group so they could draw strength for this transition time. Following a daily prescription of breath work and guided meditation, they were able to achieve a sense of calmness and understanding that comforted them both. Sidney and Caroline were then able to free their minds from stressful thoughts and make the most of their remaining time together.

Fear of death is extremely common. The root of this fear stems from a variety of factors, including fear of the unknown, fear of going to hell, fear of ceasing to exist, loss of control, and the desire to continue an active physical life.

To help release a fear of dying, remember that this world is not our home; we are merely travelers passing through. We entered this world empty-handed and alone, and we will leave empty-handed and alone. Everything we accumulated in this life, including our physical body and possessions, will be left behind. All we can take with us are the imprints of the positive and negative actions we created.

Rx #97: If we embrace death as the final letting go and leave a legacy of positive deeds, thoughts, and emotions, we can move to our next phase with the lightness of being which is called enlightenment.

Rx #98: There is nothing more important than the breath. It keeps us alive until the final moment of our lives. It gives us a feeling of calm, even in the midst of turmoil. The breath comes and goes. Observe it and don't get too attached to the process.

Meditation is another proven stress reliever. Quieting the mind, breathing and letting go of tension stored in the body, allows you to gain control of your life. When thoughts or feelings arise during meditation, do not try to erase them. Do not worry or analyze them. Do not be frightened or sad. These emotions are like the clouds passing overhead. Accept them as part of life. Nothing stays the same; when your mind stops its chatter, your higher self will tell you what needs to be done.

Chet called one day to tell me that he'd been feeling torn between his budding career and his family. "I went for a long walk and I heard my little voice telling me to move to Nashville as clear and loud as though it was coming over a loudspeaker," he said. "I told my wife. She agreed and we began making plans to relocate." The family adjusted and Chet is happy playing with a band and writing songs.

When we encounter stressful or fearful situations, we feel as though we have no control, which leads to anxiety and a sense of powerlessness. We feel like victims and our strength is stripped away. When we feel we have no control over our lives, depression slips in and joy evaporates.

You have the ability to make things different by gaining control of your life and erasing your irrational fears.

Start with the breath. I cannot repeat this too many times. Just do it. Breathe. Meditate in a quiet place. Meditation is a chance to be with you totally. It doesn't have to be on a mountain or under ideal conditions. It can be in a meadow or a garage. Meditation is a lifestyle change. The objective is to set aside time each day to keep your mind quiet and get rid of fears that overwhelm your natural joyful state.

Meditation means tapping into your own essence – learning to be happy with who you are. It can also help you find the creative voice and serene sense of well-being that we all crave.

Rx #99: Developing a meditation practice is one of the best remedies for anxiety.

Some call it the elixir of well-being; others attribute it to their increase in self-esteem and inner calm. Although meditation requires both discipline and consistency, it is worth the commitment; doctors are now documenting the positive results of meditation on both physical and mental health.

After you have calmly and objectively looked at what is bothering you, you can list the fears that have been limiting your life. I suggest making a list of five fears that keep you in a heightened stress state. Once you have done that you can consciously get a grip on what is making you miserable and stressed. It is then that you can start letting go of the tension in your life. You'll be surprised at how this exercise can defuse stress levels – you might even wonder how you were uptight for so long.

The final stage in this process is to adopt a relaxed way of looking at life. I also recommend addressing troublesome issues so you can start to remedy them. One thing to note is that worry and stress do little to change problems. That's why they are known to be one of the most wasted of emotions.

When you are able to find a peaceful calm place amidst the chaos, you will have achieved stress-free living.

The Bodhi Tree Breath Meditation

The bodhi tree is an ancient sacred fig tree. Siddhartha Gautama, the spiritual teacher and founder of Buddhism, sat under the bodhi tree while achieving enlightenment. It is said that Gautama spent a whole week in front of the bodhi tree at the Mahabodhi Temple with his eyes fixated on the Supreme Being.

You don't have to stand in front of a bodhi tree with unwavering faith to attain inner peace. You simply have to breathe. The breath is always with us. We don't have to buy, borrow or invent it. You can breathe anywhere, anytime. Your breath is the vehicle that brings the body and mind into balance. It can also minimize the internal chatter that can wreak havoc on your central nervous system.

When you feel yourself being gripped by fear, pay attention to your breath. Be mindful of the moments when you aren't breathing. Pay attention to how deeply you are breathing, and notice the energy boost you get when you breathe properly. Your breath has the ability to calm your mind and stop its mindless chatter.

There are probably moments when no air is going in or coming out of your lungs. When this happens your body can become oxygen deprived. When that happens, thoughts can get muddled and you might feel disoriented. In extreme cases you can lose consciousness or faint. Some people stop breathing while they sleep. This potentially lethal condition is called sleep apnea. (If you suspect you have it, see a doctor immediately).

Most of us take in small amounts of air when we breathe. Most of the oxygen that we take into our lungs is dispensed into the blood stream through the lower lungs. Yet we avoid these deep, blood-enriched breaths that pull air down to the bronchial tubes and fill up the lungs. With mindful deep breathing you are filling the body with oxygen while preventing a state of tension.

Experiencing Joyful Living

The Southwest coast of Florida is made up of 10,000 islands. Each year a large number of outdoor enthusiasts flock there to fish, kayak and photograph nature's beauty. To the uneducated eye the islands all look the same, which is why visitors can easily get lost. The individual with an inquiring eye, however, is quick to notice subtle differences which characterize each island.

Like an island, each of us is completely unique. Knowing this truth allows us to navigate our earthly path with confidence. But how do we progress? Going back to the island analogy, it might be prudent to use a compass.

A magnetic compass must be adjusted to provide an accurate course of direction. Likewise, we may deviate from our path as we progress through life, making necessary corrections when we tune into our heart center. By listening to your inner compass, the intuitive voice within, you will never be lost. Instead, you will always have an inner mechanism to show you the correct journey.

The successes of one's journey can never be measured by outsiders. I cannot measure yours, nor can you measure mine. I cannot see what is right for you because we have different lessons to learn and paths to follow that lead us to our highest good.

Your perception of success is determined by what is true north for you. The footprint each of us casts in the sand cannot be duplicated or changed in any way.

Success cannot (and should not) be measured by material possessions. Life is not about fancy clothes, grand living or expensive cars. It's about who we are and the mark we leave on society. The most successful and admired people were often recognized as successful because they believed in themselves; Ghandi in his homespun clothing, Buddha sitting beneath the bodhi tree, Mother Teresa serving the poor.

Like them, our success might be found in helping others (or being selfless). The illusion of success based on job position, salary and possessions just inflates ones ego. It becomes a mirage that prevents people from knowing who they really are and what their purpose is on Earth. If you dig within yourself – and discover what moves you and makes your life worthwhile – then you will feel rich beyond all measure.

Rx #100: Be OK with who you are. Stop trying to be someone else.

Follow your intuitive star and you will find success. It is said that it is better to do your own dharma poorly then someone else's well. This means you have to follow your own path, do your own duties, don't try to become someone you are not or take on the life that is not yours.

From time to time we all visit a place of inertia when we can't seem to get motivated. Making a decision is not always an easy task, and often we avoid making decisions out of fear.

Sometimes we have to stay with the feeling of being stuck until it melts away. At other times, we may have to break through uncertainty with force. This is done by leveraging yourself and changing directions. It is also important to learn to cope with paralyzing fear that holds you back from being the best person you can be.

By incorporating the meditation and breathing exercises in this book and on my website, www.stressreduction.com you will reduce stress and anxiety. Keeping a journal can also be an effective tool to finding your North Star and creating harmony in your life. It has been known to help rid people of negative thoughts and generate positive ones instead. By exercising your power of mindfulness and awareness, you will build a solid foundation for growth. Once you are standing in that power you will find that inertia has lost its hold on you.

Rx #101: Remember: Whatever the mind can conceive, the body can achieve. That's your power.

All behavior changes require dedication, commitment, discipline and a pledge to move forward, whether you are letting go of cigarettes, overeating, or need to correct a relationship. Over the years I've found that resistance can stop progress. If you are not willing to make life-altering changes, you will find reasons not to progress and you will avoid meditation and wallow in the status quo.

If you don't want to change right now that's fine. But just reading this book indicates that you are ready (and willing) to make positive changes. While the value of stress-reducing techniques comes from the practicing, start at a pace you are comfortable with. Don't beat yourself up if you can't find the time or the motivation to make all the changes that you want.

It will come when you are ready. Remember, there are no magic pills or mystical fixes for your life or anyone else's. You, and only you, can reduce your stress levels. You have all the instruments at your disposal, wherever you are and at all times.

When you meditate you may fall asleep, or you may be disturbed by mindless chatter in your head. You may start and stop, or you may not start at all. When you do begin, do not become attached to the outcome. That only adds more stress. Instead, use the exercises and meditations as practice. Like the Master Archer, I can only guide you to the path of less stress. I cannot make you do it if you are not ready.

Rx #102: There is no right or wrong way to meditate. Accept what you are offered and be happy with only a few minutes a day. With time you can and will increase your time and your enjoyment of the process. The important thing is: DO NOT GIVE UP. Keep sitting in the stillness as often as possible. It is the answer you have been looking for and the antidote to fear and stress.

In the Golden Moment meditation (see page 100) we are perfect beings perceiving an imperfect world that is perfect. This is a basic truth. We have all the wisdom inside ourselves to become happy and live a relatively stress-free life. We simply need to use the innate intelligence and wisdom we already possess.

Sometimes the best thing to do is nothing. Stay quiet, just be, and pay attention to everything around you. The answer to all your questions will come when you are calm and ready to receive. I wish you well on your journey to relaxation.

Rx #103: Death will come soon enough. Life is about living.

Serendipity, in which people and circumstances converge in an unlikely, unplanned and highly unpredictable manner, is peculiar. But throughout our lives we encounter unusual situations and people for a reason. Some stay with us; others fade away over time and are never seen again. We can choose to receive and accept without resistance things that we may not rationally understand. We can be like the butterfly that dances with the wind – playfully and easily. To do so, we must surrender completely to the moment and allow ourselves to be swept into the sound of two hands clapping as one.

This surrender is the essence of a blissful existence. We do not know – nor will we ever know – what life may bring. To handle it with grace, then, is to remind ourselves again and again that "this is what is happening right now." The degree to which we can say this – and mean it, offering no resistance – determines our level of ease and happiness in life. No one's life is stress-free or perfect, but through difficulties, practice and patience we can become masters in our own right.

This is the spirit in which this book was created; may it guide you on your quest for continuing happiness and peace.

POSTSCRIPT

"Peace is Every Step" Thich Nhat Hanh

When I resumed doctoral studies in the field of mind/body medicine and integrative healthcare, little did I suspect that this path would take me to remote areas in Southern Mexico.

My studies with native shaman healers put me on the path to self-discovery. I received wisdom that was passed down from generation to generation on healing illness and disease with herbs, intuition and ceremony.

In that environment a new world opened up to me. What I discovered was a vast country rich in culture, warmth and compassion. I met happy people who see every day as a celebration. I also discovered a healthcare system steeped in century's old wisdom that combined empathy and ritual, rather than pharmaceutical drugs.

I was particularly intrigued by the Chaya plant, and now seven years after discovering its healing properties, Dr. Chaya organic nutritional bars and energy drinks will soon be available. Information about these and other products are on my website, www.stressreduction.com.

You'll also find my Guided Body Scan Meditation CD and Healing Chi Kung DVD. These unique relaxation tools are worth the nominal investment if you cannot attend one of my clinics or healing journeys. It will, however, put you in a deep state of relaxation where your intuitive self can share insights about your deepest anxieties and innermost longings.

I offer week-long Stress Reduction Vacations in the tropical mountains of central Mexico. The indigenous people consider this region to be sacred, and so do I. Tourists who have visited always say the vibrational level there is unparalleled. Each time I return I'm left with a sense of ease and awe. My stress vanishes and the world seems light and happy.

My programs will bring you this same inner peace and light that so many of us crave. The Stress Reduction Vacations are an opportunity for you to reach your optimal level of mental, emotional, physical and spiritual nirvana. Participation is limited to small groups to maintain intimacy and individual attention. This is not just a workshop – it's an adventure.

Visit www.stressreduction.com for more information.

The Solution to the Nine Dots

In chapter Four I asked you to connect nine dots with four continuous lines, without lifting your pencil from the paper. Did you figure it out?

Chances are you tried to go around the perimeter. But that left the one dot in the center. What we learned here is that we are so conditioned to think in our old ways that we tend to look for similar (and easy) solutions to new problems. The lesson is to think creatively. Trying to figure out this game will show you how to think outside the box. In other words, it will help you find alternative solutions to situations where you feel you are stuck.

The answer:

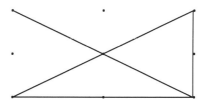

103 Prescriptions for Overcoming Stress and Achieving Lifelong Happiness

Rx #1: Whatever the mind can conceive, the body can usually achieve. Even if you are riddled with pain and are stressed out, you can learn to be peaceful, pain-free and relaxed once you've mastered a few simple techniques.

RX #2: Here is a mini-meditation. Remain in the NOW. Don't try to second guess what's coming at you in the next five seconds, and stop worrying about the past. Let it go. Be here. Be in the NOW. Gently close your eyes. Now breathe. Watch your breath. Feel your chest expand with each inhale and contract with each exhale. Everything is always perfect in the present moment. Breathe again and relax your shoulders. There's nothing you can do to change the past and the future does not exist in the present.

Rx #3: Crying is an appropriate response when stress becomes unbearable. So when you feel the urge, let it out. Let the tears fly and don't bottle up your stress where it can wreak havoc on your body and make you ill.

Rx #4: Reduce stress by accepting the situations in your life as they are in this moment – and I mean every aspect of them. Stop thinking about what should be happening or who you think you should be.

Rx #5: SLOW DOWN. When you rush from one thing to the next, you set yourself up for more stress.

Rx #6: With eating disorders, as with any recovery process, there must be a lifestyle change. And only YOU can make that change.

Rx #7: You and only YOU are responsible for your own well-being. Only YOU can make yourself sick or well, heavy or slender. It's all up to you. Only YOU can take responsibility for your own actions. No one is forcing you to overeat – you made that decision and that means you have the power to reverse that decision.

Rx #8: For every concept that holds you back – beating yourself up for past mistakes is a big one – there is a recipe for true healing: Relax into the present moment and leave the past behind.

Rx #9: Making a decision and sticking to it will empower you to reach your goals. There is nothing the human mind cannot accomplish, provided there is the drive or willpower. And the better you feel, the more you will accomplish.

Rx #10: Change is difficult. So make ONE behavioral correction each day and do not worry about tomorrow. You know why – because tomorrow always takes care of itself.

Rx #11: Unless you are willing to take responsibility for your life (all of it) you will continue to be stuck where you are now. If you want to change the outcome you must change what is happening inside of you. That means being diligent about the life choices you make, the relationships you encounter, the food you eat and the exercise you do (or don't do). If you don't do that, you will remain stuck where you are. If your intent is to lose weight, then you must eat mindfully.

Rx #12: You wouldn't buy a house or a car without knowing the price. So why would you put food in your mouth without knowing what it's going to cost you in calories and potential extra weight?

Rx #13: Pay attention to what your body needs and fuel up with healthful food, not junk food.

Rx #14: Take control of your eating habits by following the suggestions above. Eat healthy foods and smaller portions, know the emotional price of the foods you eat, avoid skipping meals and eating late in the evening, and put down your fork when you're full.

Rx #15: Do the Raisin Trick whenever you feel stressed, anxious or sad and you feel compelled to eat.

Rx #16: Anything of a sexual nature that puts you outside your comfort level is a topic for discussion with your partner. You need not let anyone shame, humiliate, or push you into doing something you don't want to do just to save the relationship.

Rx #17: Taking risks and being spontaneous in sex can stimulate sexual growth and open new vistas, or it can backfire. Explore what works best for you and your partner.

Rx #18: Slow down. Don't rush through the sexual act. Foreplay, stroking, cuddling and kissing will lead to more satisfactory lovemaking for both parties.

Rx #19: It takes a lot of patience to be a successful lover, and it's an active process that can take years to perfect. Most successful lovers enjoy pleasing their partners and want to know how to do so.

Rx #20: To build intimacy, start by opening the lines of communication. Share a desire and encourage your partner to do the same. Studies have shown that telling your partner what you want in bed leads to deeper emotional intimacy. Enjoy time together without interruptions, both in and out of the bedroom, to promote a connection.

Rx #21: A man wants a partner who accepts him even when he cannot perform. So if things don't go as planned, don't make a big deal about it or get stressed. Make him feel emotionally safe, even when he has trouble performing. This is true for both partners, inside and outside the bedroom. Feeling accepted for one's faults and failures is what builds intimacy and keeps it in place.

Rx #22: Boring sex is a death sentence when it comes to passion. Keep the spark alive with spontaneity, new ideas, positions, locations, or the use of magazines or X-rated movies. Anything that takes both of you away from the sexual routine and into something new and exciting will invigorate your sexual experience.

Rx #23: Nobody is perfect – not even the airbrushed models in the men's magazines. So lighten up!

Rx #24: The best sex is the result of open communication. If you are experiencing a problem with your partner, talk about it – but not in the bedroom. Don't hide under the covers and pretend it's not there, because problems don't simply disappear. If you cannot resolve the situation, seek professional help with a therapist or sex counselor.

Rx #25: Sexual stress is usually a symptom of other conflicts within the partnership. Instead of being afraid to deal with your anger, learn to keep it out of your relationship. For example, if your boss is giving you grief, don't let it seep into your bedroom. Find ways to diffuse the issues with your boss so that you can enjoy your partner.

Rx #26: Moments that seem important at the time are often just a blip on the screen of eternal life. So let negativity go and forgive conflicts without judgment, allowing the conflict to dissipate into nothingness.

Rx #27: Ask for what you want. Asking does not guarantee you will get it, but it certainly improves your chances. Show or tell your lover what things excite you the most. If your partner needs convincing, take baby steps toward your ultimate goal.

Rx #28: There is no past or future. There is only the now! Live in the moment.

Rx #29: Take responsibility for your situation. Get into a quiet place to find a solution for promoting your own personal wellness.

Rx #30: You cannot allow others to rob you of your happiness.

Rx #31: Try not to attach emotional or mental baggage to events that are insignificant in the larger scheme of things. Let the past stay in the past and start each minute anew.

Rx 32: Only you can save yourself; no one can do it for you. You are the only one who can change a situation and actualize your dreams.

Rx #33: Imagine your worst fear, and then find a remedy before it happens. Know what you should do in advance so you can move into action quickly. Having a plan will immediately reduce your stress so you'll be ready for the emergency if one occurs.

Rx #34: Unpleasant situations and toxic people cause anxieties. Some things cannot be changed, so change must come from within.

Rx #35: Since conflict causes stress, you must find a way to deal with the situation without causing more stress on your system.

Rx #36: There is no trick to meditating, but there is a reward. Total relaxation is your birthright. We all deserve to be at rest. And remember, a body that can find a place of rest wants to return to that place of rest.

Rx #37: You cannot change others, so learn to accept them. Stay in the moment and know that everything is alright now.

Rx #38: There is no reason to give someone else the power to determine whether you are going to have a good day or a bad day.

Rx #39: No matter how competent and wonderful you are, it's impossible to please everybody. So stop trying. Do your job and let other people's nastiness roll off your back.

Rx #40: Recognize that the other people's problems are theirs. Don't make them yours and don't take them personally.

Rx #41: A smile, a compliment and a kind word goes a long way in making a less stressful work environment. A positive attitude diffuses negativity and cuts through them personally.

Rx #42: Don't gossip or spread rumors. Keep confidential information to yourself. Respect the privacy of others. Remember: Great minds discuss ideas, mediocre minds discuss events, and small minds discuss people.

Rx #43: Believe it or not, getting fired or leaving a job because of stress usually turns out to be a blessing in disguise.

Rx #44: Know how office politics can affect you. Learn who has power and clout and make nice – or at least stay under their radar.

Rx #45: Refrain from speaking or acting before hearing all the facts. Stop wasting your time and energy on what you think may have happened. There may be a perfectly good explanation for a particular action. Ask for it.

Rx #46: Hold yourself accountable for your mistakes and failures instead of making excuses and blaming others. Also, take credit for your successes and contributions.

Rx #47: No one can make you feel a certain way. You have the power to respond, so don't give that power away. Keep in mind that YOU are in charge of your emotions, and YOU determine the amount of stress you experience in your life.

Rx #48: We can take personal responsibility and create an exciting and dynamic life instead of staying in a miserable situation and making ourselves sick. Regardless of our chronological age, we have free will. This is our birthright.

Rx #49: Listen to your heart as well as your body. What your gut tells you to do is always correct. Be willing to leave toxic work situations before they create illness. Life is too short, so why use it up in a work environment that makes you unhappy or sick? Remember, you have free will.

Rx #50: The choice to work for others or to be self-employed is yours to make. Weigh the pros and cons of both – then trust in yourself. You can succeed in anything you choose if you have a dream and the desire to do so.

Rx #51: If there is a toxic situation or person who is a problem, you might want to consider cutting ties and releasing the stress it's causing.

Rx #52: You can cling to your tension, or you can release it. It's up to you whether to be stressed or relaxed.

Rx #53: Letting go means giving up fear, control, old habits, guilt, regrets and voices from the past. It means living in the present.

Rx #54: It takes a leap of faith and a positive can-do attitude to jump off the cliff and know you'll land on your feet. Only fear holds you back.

Rx #55: Worry adds to stress. It makes you crazy over something that may never happen.

Rx #56: Worry is like a bag of bricks. You can put it down at any time.

Rx #57: Lighten up. Live your life with integrity and let others live theirs: don't force anyone to comply with your rules, wishes or demands.

Rx #58: In order to let go of stress and anxiety rooted in your childhood, let go of your preoccupation of looking for someone to blame (usually a parent) and focus on love and forgiveness. Remember: Everyone really is doing the best that they can.

Rx #59: Anything that constricts our throats also restricts our ability to communicate because it separates the head from the heart.

Rx #60: When you find yourself being pulled in diverging directions, begin letting go of stress by paying attention to what you are doing. Be mindful of the things that create tension. Figure out if there is a way to substitute a more pleasant, less stressful, activity. If not, choose to enjoy some aspect of what you are doing, even if you are not satisfied.

Rx #61: There is always room to make new (and better) choices. However, it will mean letting go of the things that are holding you back from enjoying your time here on this planet.

Rx #62: Once you discover the hidden source of your dissatisfaction, you can start opening up your mind to release it, like butterflies leaving a net.

Rx #63: You are in charge. You are the master of your own well-being. All options you need for optimal health are at your disposal. It is within your power to unblock the deep layers of stress and peel them away. You have the ability to reduce the daily worries that sap your strength and vitality. Until you realize this, you may not live up to your maximum potential.

Rx #64: It's up to you to set limits. If you allow others to push you around, you have no one to blame but yourself. Stand up for yourself. Stop playing the victim!

Rx #65: What happened in the past, or will occur in the future, is not important; what is important is the NOW.

Rx #66: Every individual must create a method of winding down and relaxing. This quest must be done on a daily basis to maintain balance in this ever-challenging world.

Rx #67: Becoming aware of the world inside yourself is a powerful way for you to let go of stressors in life. Forgiveness of oneself and others is payment in full. We then become Masters in the Art of Letting Go.

Rx #68: When you think about your life, can you see the upside to a downside situation? Can you enjoy the Golden Moments of your life?

Rx #69: When you are truly present you're in the Golden Moment. That's the perfect place to be. In the present there is no pain of the past or fear of the future.

Rx #70: It is fine to take a risk. In fact, it's often a good thing. But reality must play a part in this interface. You wouldn't jump out of an airplane without a parachute, so you must differentiate between logical intuition and irrational action. To make sure you know the difference you must listen to the voice within.

Rx #71: The only thing holding you back from achieving your wildest dreams is you. Rewards are reaped when we trust our inner voice enough to take risks. The unknown can be the firecracker that sparks the fortune of tomorrow. Make sure you remember that.

Rx #72: Focus on the positive, rather than the negative, and the fear of the unknown will lose its iron grip.

Rx #73: No-win situations are only in your mind. Life is win-win as long as you take a breath and realize how glorious it is that you are alive. And that means that your possibilities are endless.

Rx #74: Open your mind to the wisdom of your intuition. Allow yourself to face your fears and anxieties so you can address them and let them go. There is no time like the present to face your fears and deal with them.

Rx #75: You can design your own path to mental, emotional and spiritual wellness. You don't have to follow anyone else's lead.

Rx #76: Familiarize yourself with the language of money, which is a tangible source of energy.

Rx #77: Irrational fear can interfere with normal functioning. This interference will upset your equilibrium and place you at a health risk.

Rx #78: Always assume you are in good health and focus on the positive functioning of your body. If you have a specific health problem that needs attention, see a medical professional.

Rx #79: Living in fear that you will become ill is one sure way to missing out on the beauty of your life right now. The now is all we have at this moment. So why waste it worrying about the maybe?

Rx #80: It is always helpful to focus on the positive side of your goals.

Rx #81: Success is a creative dynamic entity that can upset the apple cart. It may create a sense of guilt and feelings that you don't deserve it. That's why healthy self-esteem is a good thing to have before you chase your dreams. The reason is that you have to step out of your comfort zone and face any doubts that prevent you from achieving happiness and success.

Rx #82: Examine the degree to which you can create your own joyful experiences. Be aware that too much dependence on others can undermine your confidence in yourself, and cause a greater fear of rejection.

Rx #83: To overcome the fear of rejection you must define yourself in a way that doesn't make you dependent on what others think of you.

Rx #84: The greater your attachment to a significant other, the greater your fear of rejection might be.

Rx #85: To prevent an emotional roller-coaster ride with your partner, don't plan the future prematurely. Always know that the relationship may not work out, so be sure to have a hobby, activities, and friends outside the relationship that bring you joy.

Rx #86: Remember, you are as old as you feel. It's best to live your life making the most of your physical and mental abilities. If you feel old you will be old, if you feel young, you will be young (age is just a number, remember?)

Rx #87: To challenge your fears about living and dying, try to change the order and pattern of your daily existence. Take a different route to work, shop at a different grocery store, or eat on a different schedule. Be spontaneous – get out of your rut.

Rx #88: Training the mind to focus on things you have control over – and letting go of things that are impossible to change – are the best antidotes to anxiety and phobias.

Rx #89: Fear makes people feel isolated and alone, yet it is part of the growth process. When we feel alone we become more compassionate with ourselves and others. In facing our fears we become fearless warriors.

Rx #90: Don't be intimidated by money. If you need help managing money or balancing your checkbook, ask for it. Become conscious when you are handling money and you will become more comfortable with your finances. Forget get-rich-quick-schemes, however. They are usually just that – schemes.

Rx #91: Make it a habit to fill your mind with thoughts of happiness and safety.

Rx #92: Break your worry habits one step at a time.

Rx #93: Success comes from within, not from outside. Taking risks in life and following our intuition are mandatory to evolve and discover true happiness. Know the difference between intuitive action and irrational behavior. The wrong choice usually comes from running away from the self.

Rx #94: The less confident you are about being able to create a happy relationship, the more likely you will pick someone who will not treat you well.

Rx #95: Maintaining close ties to family and friends reduces the fear of being alone. Even if you don't have a significant other, surround yourself with people you like, or join social activities to promote good mental and physical health.

Rx #96: Try to set aside your fears and anxieties and welcome the journey ahead. Embrace the gift of aging with a positive attitude.

Rx #97: If we embrace death as the final letting go and leave a legacy of positive deeds, thoughts, and emotions, we can move to our next phase with the lightness of being which is called enlightenment.

Rx #98: There is nothing more important than the breath. It keeps us alive until the final moment of our lives. It gives us a feeling of calm, even in the midst of turmoil. The breath comes and goes. Observe it and don't get too attached to the process.

Rx #99: Developing a meditation practice is one of the best remedies for anxiety.

Rx #100: Be OK with who you are. Stop trying to be someone else.

Rx #101: Remember: Whatever the mind can conceive, the body can achieve. That's your power.

Rx #102: There is no right or wrong way to meditate. Accept what you are offered and be happy with only a few minutes a day. With time you can and will increase your time and your enjoyment of the process. The important thing is DO NOT GIVE UP. Keep sitting in the stillness as often as possible. It is the answer you have been looking for and the antidote to fear and stress.

Rx #103: Death will come soon enough. Life is about living.

Made in the USA
Charleston, SC
11 May 2014